home living workbooks

lampshades

home living workbooks

lampshades

Katrin Cargill

photography by **James Merrell**

Clarkson Potter/Publishers
New York

Originally published in Great Britain in 1996 by Ryland Peters & Small.

Published by Clarkson N. Potter/Publishers, 201 East 50th Street, New York, New York 10022. Member of the Crown Publishing Group.

Random House, Inc. New York, Toronto, London, Sydney, Auckland.

http://www.randomhouse.com/

CLARKSON N. POTTER, POTTER, and colophon are trademarks of Clarkson N. Potter, Inc.

Printed in Hong Kong

Library of Congress Cataloging-in-Publication Data is available upon request.

ISBN 0-517-70671-7

10 9 8 7 6 5 4 3 2 1

First American Edition

  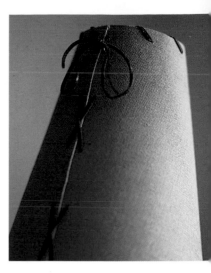

contents

once you start looking at people's lamps and what they put on them, you quickly realize that the lampshade is one of the last things to be considered in a room. Get the walls right, buy the furniture, get a mortgage for the curtains, maybe find a good lamp base or two and that's it; most people have run out of steam. So it's time to give the poor lampshade a thought or two. Most people's solution is a quick trip to a department store for a supply of cardboard shades, which are usually the wrong size for the lamps. I can't walk into a room any more without being drawn instantly to what's on the lamps, and our own house now has an ever-changing array of prototypes in different fabrics.

The mood of a room can be instantly changed by the addition of the right lampshade, the right light, and the right amount of it. New technology in lighting has meant that not only can you control your environment better with lighting, but dotting around a few well-chosen lamps and shades can create little areas of coziness and interest within a room. Color schemes can be enhanced with the right shade; a silk taffeta shade, for example, can add a touch of real luxury. Shapes are an area to look at – mostly we get the standard cone or Empire shape, when perhaps a tapered box shape would best suit the base. This book is full of ideas for shapes and sizes, trimmings and fabrics to inspire you to remedy that all-too-often neglected part of home decorating, and there are clear step-by-step instructions for making your own lampshades. You will also find, as I did, that there are a surprising number of skilled lampshade makers around who make some of the ideas shown in the book.

Katrin Cargill

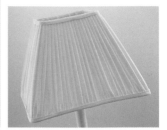

left A three-dimensional pinch-pleated ruffle border sits on the widely flaring rim of a bowed oval shade (seen in full opposite), emphasizing the exaggerated curve.
below Gathered silk covers a basic square frame.

shapes

Lampshades come in all manner of shapes, and the outline of the basic frame is what gives the shade its intrinsic character. There are plenty of shapes to choose from – including drums and cylinders; cones of all sorts, from the more open Empire and shallow cone to the tall narrow chimney; bowed shades with a concave profile; or more solid looking straight-sided shades which may be hexagonal or more box-like, in the form of a gently tapering square or rectangle.

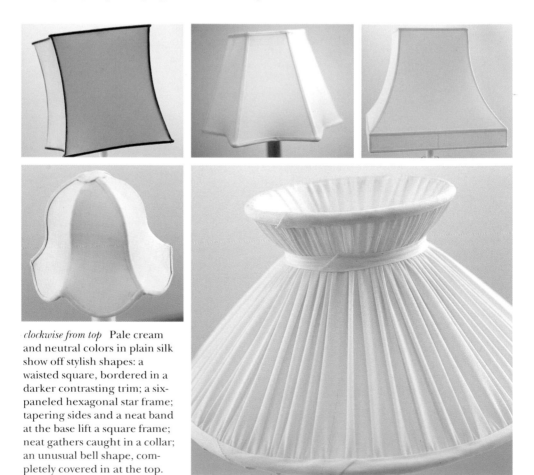

clockwise from top Pale cream and neutral colors in plain silk show off stylish shapes: a waisted square, bordered in a darker contrasting trim; a six-paneled hexagonal star frame; tapering sides and a neat band at the base lift a square frame; neat gathers caught in a collar; an unusual bell shape, completely covered in at the top.

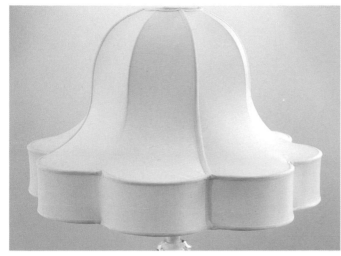
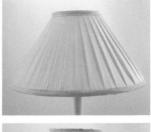

clockwise from top An impressively large covered bell shade with a deeply banded base – a sturdy frame and a very pretty shape for a floor lamp; the standard cone shape, like this gathered shade, works in any size, for floors or for tables; a wide bowed oval with a narrow waist and a ruffled edge (detail shown opposite); a collared Empire shade, finished with a plain band at the top and bottom and around the collar; pleated cotton flares out from a narrow circular opening at the top to a wider square base; a basic straight-sided Empire shade shows off tightly gathered silk to its best effect.

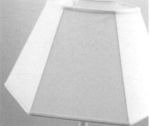

clockwise from top This elegant wavy edged frame is covered in tightly-pleated silk; an octagonal oblong shape with a Regency feel; a wide hexagonal shade allows plenty of light to shine out – ideal for a floor lamp; a wide mushroom-shaped cone; neat wide box pleats fan out over an elongated oval shade.

laminated
checked square

Cheerful red and white check linen is laminated to produce a stiff,
square-sided shade that will add a touch of color to any setting. If you
use a large-checked fabric, try to position the pattern so the checks are
centered along the folded edges for a look of symmetry; with
smaller-scale patterns the positioning is not as important.

materials & equipment

2-inch square wire frame

6-inch square wire frame, with gimbal

⅛ yard checked linen, 45 inches wide

cardboard for template

10 inches self-adhesive lampshade backing, 45 inches wide

fabric glue

metal straightedge

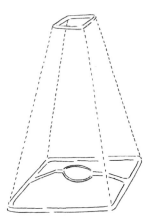

1 Start by making a cardboard template for the shade. Draw one face measuring 10 inches in height, 6 inches across the bottom, and 2 inches across the top.

2 Use the template and a pencil to mark the shape of the shade on the self-adhesive backing. Draw one face first and flip the template over to mark the other three with adjoining edges. Draw pencil lines to indicate the folded edges of the shade. Add a ½-inch seam allowance at one side. Cut one piece.

3 Position the backing over the wrong side of the fabric with the pattern on the bias. Peel off the paper and smooth the backing over the fabric.

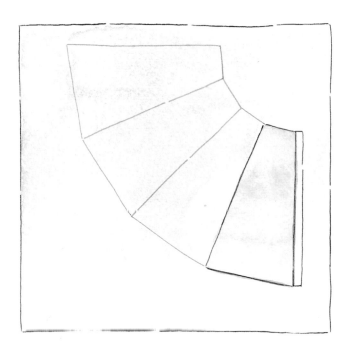

4 Cut out the laminated fabric, adding an extra ⅛-inch of linen along the side without a seam allowance. Fold this flap onto the backing and glue it in position.

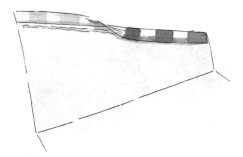

pleated silk

A buttery yellow silk taffeta is tightly pleated all around the top of this small cone, so the pleats fan out evenly around the gently flaring sides for a crisp, clean effect. The lamp is then given a punchy finish with scarlet trimming around the top and bottom rings in the same rich fabric as the main body of the shade, for a strong contrast. The inner silk lining protects the outer cover and gives the whole design a highly professional finish.

materials & equipment

cone frame with six struts and base gimbal fitting: 4-inch diameter top; 10-inch diameter bottom; 5-inch height

⅜ yard silk lining, 45 inches wide

⅜ yard butter-yellow silk taffeta, 60 inches wide

3 x 36-inch strip of red silk taffeta

½-inch-wide binding tape

basic sewing kit (see page 98)

5 Place the laminated fabric right side down on a flat surface. Using the outside edge of the blade of a pair of scissors and a metal straightedge, score along the pencil lines (made in step 2) marking the four sides of the shade.

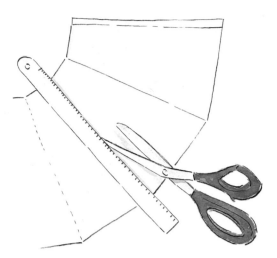

6 Use the scored lines to create sharp folds at the edges of the shade. To join it up, fold the seam allowance at a 90° angle and run some fabric glue down the linen side. Press it to the opposite straight edge, on the inside, and hold until set.

7 To assemble the shade, glue around the bottom inside edge of the shade and the outside edge of the gimbal frame. Insert the frame and hold it in place until set (clothespins are handy for holding the frame in position). Repeat for the top frame.

8 To trim the shade and hide the raw edges, make up 34 inches of ½-inch-wide bias binding from the linen fabric (see Techniques, page 103). Cut it into two strips for the top and bottom, one measuring 9 inches and the other, 25 inches. Run fabric glue along the inside of the binding strips and attach to the top and bottom of the shade, beginning at the seam and folding them over the edges as you go. Where the ends meet, turn under one raw edge and stick it down so that it neatly overlaps the other raw edge. Set the shade on a small base and use a 40-watt golfball bulb.

6 Hemstitch (see Techniques, page 102) the pleats to the top binding and trim. Repeat the pleating for the bottom edge, fanning the pleats out a little to fit the wider base. Pin and hemstitch as before.

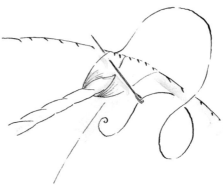

7 Slip the lining casing inside the frame with the wrong side against the taffeta and the seams aligned with the side struts. Make small snips to allow for the gimbal arms. Pin around the top and bottom of the frame so the fabric is tight and evenly stretched all around. Hemstitch in place and trim.

8 To finish the gimbal edges, cut three pieces of lining silk 1 x 4 inches. Fold the long edges to the middle and press. Wrap under a gimbal arm and pin and hand-sew the ends securely in place. Trim off the excess fabric.

9 To finish, cut two strips of red silk taffeta, one 1½ x 14 inches for the top ring, the other 1½ x 33 inches for the bottom ring. Fold each strip in half lengthwise and machine-stitch the short ends right sides together with a ½-inch seam allowance. Fold the long raw edges of each circle to the middle on the wrong side and press.

10 Slip the larger circle of silk binding around the base of the shade. Pin and neatly slipstitch in place (see Techniques, page 102) with a matching thread around both folded edges of the binding, aligning the seam with a gimbal arm. Repeat for the top trimming.

16

1 Start by binding the top and bottom rings of the frame and the base gimbal fitting with binding tape (see Techniques, page 101).

2 Cut out two pieces of lining on the bias (see Techniques, page 103), each 7 x 18 inches. Pin one piece to half of the outside of the frame, adjusting the pins as you pull the fabric tight. Mark the outline of the pins with a pencil to show the seam lines, before removing the silk.

3 Pin the second piece of lining to the pencil-marked one, right sides facing. Baste along the pencil lines at the sides, but reduce the width at the waist by ⅛ inch on each side for a tight fit. Machine-stitch two narrow lines down both curved edges, following the basting stitches and trim the excess material. Put the lining casing to one side.

4 To make the pleated outer cover, cut out a piece of yellow silk taffeta, measuring 7 x 60 inches. Mark the fabric into six equal sections top and bottom with small snips, but leave a ½-inch seam allowance at the two short ends.

5 Pin each marked section to a strut, top and bottom, and where the ends meet, turn in one raw edge by ½ inch and position it so that it overlaps the other raw edge. Working section by section, pin a series of narrow, even knife pleats along the top edge until the fabric lies flat all the way around the frame.

tall madras bowed oval

The irregular checks of a fresh green madras cotton sit well on the concave surface of this elegant bowed shade. The slender "waist" is emphasized by the strips of bias binding down the sides, which also neatly cover the stitching underneath. To avoid scorching the narrow sides of the shade, use a small low-watt "candle" bulb.

materials & equipment

bowed oval frame with six struts and four-armed gimbal: 8½ x 14-inch diameter bottom oval; 4½ x 8 inch diameter top oval; 14½-inch height with a narrow 6-inch "waist"

1¼ yards pale green madras cotton, 45 inches wide

⅝ yard white silk lampshade lining fabric, 45 inches wide

½-inch-wide binding tape

2 yards pale green ball fringe

tracing paper and pencil

fabric glue

basic sewing kit (see page 98)

5 To finish the gimbal edges, cut four rectangles of lining fabric, 1 x 2 inches each. For each strip, fold the long side in and then overlap the opposite side. Wrap each one under a gimbal edge and pull over the outside edge of the frame. Hand-sew to the binding tape and trim.

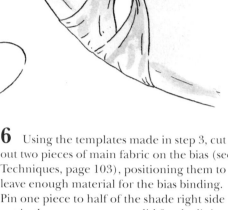

6 Using the templates made in step 3, cut out two pieces of main fabric on the bias (see Techniques, page 103), positioning them to leave enough material for the bias binding. Pin one piece to half of the shade right side out in the same way as you did for the lining. Hemstitch down both sides and along the top and bottom, sewing through the binding tape. Trim the fabric close to the stitching. Repeat this process for the other side of the frame, hemstitching through the main fabric already sewn in place.

7 Make 2¾ yards of bias binding (see Techniques, page 103) 1-inch-wide. Fold in the long edges by ¼ inch and press. Glue the binding to the two sides and around the top and bottom, tucking under and overlapping the raw ends.

8 Cut two lengths of ball fringe for the top and bottom edges and stick them in position with fabric glue. Because the shade is narrow, use a low-watt bulb.

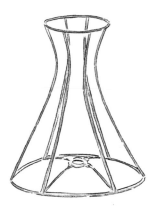

1 Bind the top and bottom ovals and the two side struts of the frame with tape (see Techniques, page 101).

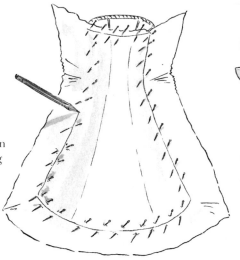

2 Cut one piece of lining fabric, larger all around than the dimensions of one half of the shade. With the wrong side out, pin it first in the middle of each side, then at the corners, and continue pinning at opposite sides around the perimeter of the shade, pulling the fabric tight as you go. Mark the outline of the pins with a pencil to show the seam line, before removing them. Trace this outline onto two pieces of paper adding a 1-inch seam allowance all around; these will be used as templates for the main fabric later on.

3 Take the remaining lining fabric and pin it to the pencil-marked piece, right sides facing. Baste along the pencil lines at the sides, but reduce the width at the waist by ½ inch on each side for a tight fit. Machine-stitch two narrow lines down both curved edges, following the basting stitches and trim the seam allowance.

4 Insert the lining inside the frame, with the raw edges facing out and pin to each corner of the frame.

Where the gimbal struts join the bottom ring, cut out small notches of fabric.

Hemstitch (see Techniques, page 102) the lining to the binding tape around the top and bottom, pulling the fabric tight, and trim the fabric close to the stitches.

above Neat knife pleats of cream silk with a silk fringe: the tops of the threads peep out above the braid to form an intriguing scalloped edging. *right from top* Cotton ticking stripes meet perfectly across the angle of this paneled shade to form a chevron design; a lightweight cotton is dipped in fabric stiffener and then diagonally draped over an Empire shade for a ruched effect; rich red crushed velvet is stiffened with lamination and trimmed in leather thonging; the finest ecru silk is tightly gathered around a cone shade and finished with a pinked skirt; moiré silk in contrasting colors is an ideal choice to complement the shaped panels of this stylish shade.

use of fabrics and trimmings

Second only to the shape of the lampshade, the type of fabric and trimming you choose to cover the frame will dictate the overall look of the shade. For instance, the same basic cone would look very different covered in a laminated striped cloth than if you decided on a loose, skirt-like cover in a floral print. Heavy and lightweight fabrics alike can be used to decorate lampshades.

left A crisp red-and-white cotton gingham is shown to best effect on a simple Empire shape. The geometric check accentuates the perfect knife pleats, which are finished in a binding of the same checked fabric, used on the diagonal.

below from left Double pinked ruffles in a complementary fabric with a smaller motif edge this tightly gathered, printed cotton shade; delicate cream lace is generously gathered and held in place over a plain cream shade by a pretty satin ribbon tied in a bow; this unusual shade is created using a thin printed cotton which is stiffened with lamination and then scored into shaped sections – bias binding finishes the raw edges and a ribbon threaded through the scored sections pulls the shade into tight gathers to form a petal pattern along the top edge.

above A cone-shaped frame is covered in a tightly gathered printed cotton and trimmed along the bottom edge in a strongly contrasting deep cotton fringe.

right Delicate checked voile floats out from a smocked top, used as a loose cover over a collared Empire silk shade. The top and bottom edges are finished in thin red velvet piping.

skirted pictorial print

Patterned fabrics work as well as solids, particularly on loose fabric lampshades. Here a pretty red and white *toile de Jouy* is sewn into a full, pleated skirt, set off with a bold matching trim that sits on the bottom edge. The shade is given added fullness with the addition of an underskirt between the outer cover and the lining.

materials & equipment

frame with six struts and reverse gimbal fitting: 7-inch diameter top;
12-inch diameter bottom; 8-inch height

1⅜ yards lining fabric, 45 inches wide

1¼ yards toile de Jouy fabric, 60 inches wide

½-inch-wide binding tape

1½ yards coordinating trimming, 1½ inches wide

basic sewing kit (see page 98)

7 Cut a piece of *toile de Jouy* fabric measuring 11 x 80 inches; machine-stitch panels and the short ends using a 1-inch seam allowance. Turn under the raw edges on the seam allowance by ¼ inch, press and machine-stitch down (do *not* stitch through to the main panel).

8 Turn the bottom edge of the *toile de Jouy* to the right side by ¼ inch and press. Pin, baste, and machine stitch the decorative trim to the right side on the bottom edge, taking in the hem, and hiding all raw edges. Neatly tuck under the ends where they meet.

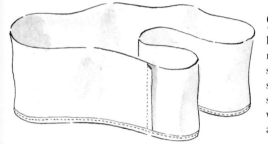

9 To line the *toile de Jouy* skirt, use a piece of lining fabric 11 x 80 inches; join panels where necessary and the short ends using a French seam (see Techniques, page 103) with a total seam allowance of 1 inch and press neatly to one side. Turn the bottom edge of the circle to the wrong side making a double ¼-inch hem; pin and machine-stitch in place.

10 Place the right side of the lining casing against the wrong side of the *toile de Jouy*. Pin and baste the raw edges of both layers together ½ inch from the top. Pin and baste a series of pleats about 1 inch wide around the top edge. Slip the skirt over the lined shade and pin around the top of the frame; make any necessary adjustments to the pleats to fit the circumference exactly. Hem-stitch in place and trim.

11 Cut a strip of *toile de Jouy* on the bias 1½ x 24 inches and machine-stitch the short ends together as in step 5. Turn under one edge by ½ inch and press. Pin the remaining raw edge to the frame, right side down and with the binding on the inside; hemstitch in place. Pull the folded edge over the frame to the outside and secure all the way around with a slipstitch (see Techniques, page 102).

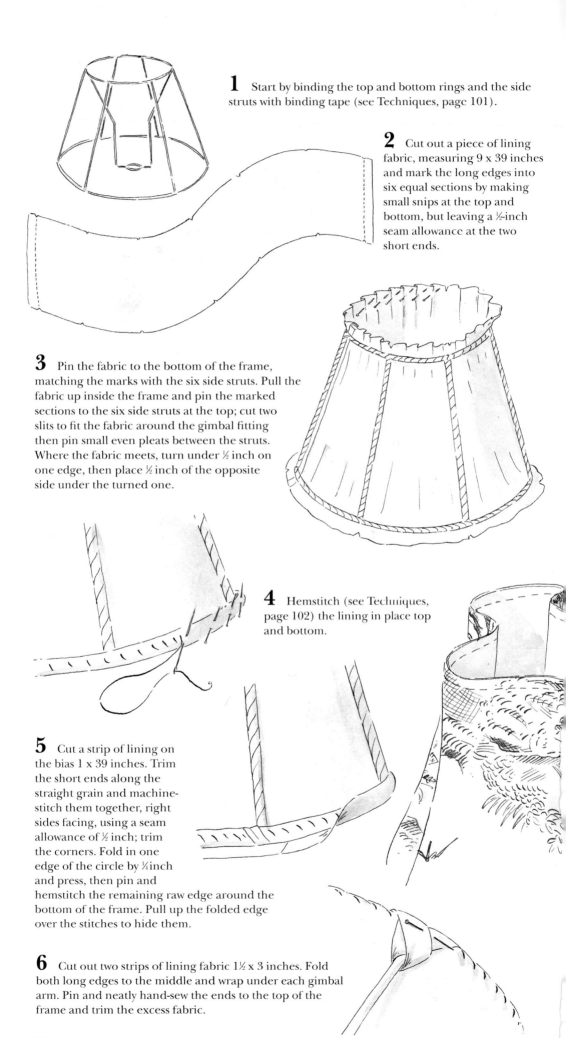

1 Start by binding the top and bottom rings and the side struts with binding tape (see Techniques, page 101).

2 Cut out a piece of lining fabric, measuring 9 x 39 inches and mark the long edges into six equal sections by making small snips at the top and bottom, but leaving a ½-inch seam allowance at the two short ends.

3 Pin the fabric to the bottom of the frame, matching the marks with the six side struts. Pull the fabric up inside the frame and pin the marked sections to the six side struts at the top; cut two slits to fit the fabric around the gimbal fitting then pin small even pleats between the struts. Where the fabric meets, turn under ½ inch on one edge, then place ½ inch of the opposite side under the turned one.

4 Hemstitch (see Techniques, page 102) the lining in place top and bottom.

5 Cut a strip of lining on the bias 1 x 39 inches. Trim the short ends along the straight grain and machine-stitch them together, right sides facing, using a seam allowance of ½ inch; trim the corners. Fold in one edge of the circle by ¼ inch and press, then pin and hemstitch the remaining raw edge around the bottom of the frame. Pull up the folded edge over the stitches to hide them.

6 Cut out two strips of lining fabric 1½ x 3 inches. Fold both long edges to the middle and wrap under each gimbal arm. Pin and neatly hand-sew the ends to the top of the frame and trim the excess fabric.

burlap half shade

Here a curvaceous, half floral shade is tightly covered with burlap. The gimp trim and coiled rope with tassels provide a decorative touch in complementary rough textures. Use a low (25-watt) bulb as the burlap has a very loose weave; if you use a higher wattage bulb, the shade should be lined.

materials & equipment

half floral frame with five struts and bulb clip: 12-inch height; 11½-inch width across top; 17-inch width across bottom; 7-inch width at waist

⅛ yard muslin, 45 inches wide

⅛ yard burlap, 45 inches wide

½-inch-wide binding tape

1¾ yards gimp braid

⅛ yard rope with tasseled ends

fabric glue

basic sewing kit (see page 98)

6 Carefully position and pin the central seam along the central strut of the frame and continue to pin all around the perimeter of the frame. Insert pins opposite each other all around the frame, pulling the burlap tight as you go.

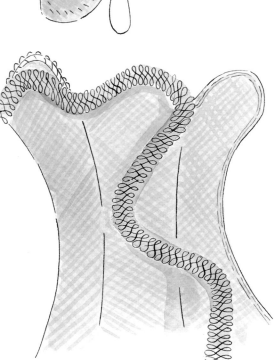

7 Once the burlap is neatly pinned in place, hemstitch (see Techniques, page 102) around the perimeter of the frame to secure. Trim off any excess fabric and frayed edges.

8 Glue the length of braid around the perimeter of the shade as a trimming and to hide the hemstitches. Fold under one raw end to overlap the other for a neat finish.

9 Finally, coil the rope trim so that both tassels hang evenly and glue the coil firmly to the central strut at the waist of the shade. If necessary, secure with a few hand stitches. Choose a bulb with a low wattage to avoid glare, or add an interlining if you prefer.

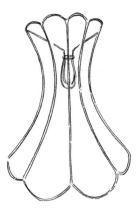

1 First bind the frame along the two outside struts, the central strut, and the top and bottom curves (see Techniques, page 101).

2 Cut the muslin in half and use one half to make a pattern. Pin the muslin to the binding tape on one half of the frame. Start pinning in the middle at the top and bottom, then pin at opposite corners, then work around the sides inserting pins as you go. Use a pencil to mark the outline made by the pins.

3 Remove the pins and marked muslin from the frame. Cut out the fabric adding an extra ½-inch seam allowance around all outside edges to make a pattern and then make a second one from the other half of the muslin. The second pattern should be a mirror image of the first.

4 Position both patterns on a square of burlap and pin in place. Make sure the patterns lie diagonally across the grain (this will give the burlap better stretch). Cut out two pieces of burlap and discard the patterns.

5 Seam the two burlap pieces together down the center using a ½-inch seam allowance. Make a double row of stitches (or strengthen with overlocking) to prevent fraying (see Techniques, page 103).

raw and ruffled

A cream raw silk is perhaps one of the most traditional and widely used lampshade coverings, providing a strong outer casing suitable for direct or indirect lighting, at the same time the rich texture of the fabric adds a sophisticated touch to any room setting. However, the shade here is given an original decorative treatment – the main body of the cone is made in laminated silk, while the top and bottom are trimmed with a double row of raw silk ruffles.

materials & equipment

4-inch diameter top ring with reversible gimbal

11-inch diameter bottom ring

1¼ yards cream raw silk, 45 inches wide

½-inch-wide binding tape

⅞ yard self-adhesive lampshade backing, 45 inches wide

paper, ruler, pencil, and tape measure

fabric glue

pinking shears

clothespins

basic sewing kit (see page 98)

6 Before sealing up the side seam, check the fit of the shade around the rings with clothespins as shown below. Mark the exact position of the overlap and remove the clothespins. Now glue the silk overlap to the opposite inside edge of the shade, lining up the marks made, and hold in place until the glue has set.

7 To assemble the shade, run a line of glue around the top and bottom inside edges of the cone and around the outside edges of both rings. Insert each ring, lining up the strips of glue, and place clothespins around the edges to hold the rings in position until the glue dries.

8 To trim the bottom edge of the shade, cut six strips of silk 34 inches long and 2 inches wide. Join them together to make two strips, each three times the length of the circumference of the bottom edge. Trim all the edges with pinking shears and lay the strips on top of one another, right sides up. Sew a line of running stitches along the middle of the strips and pull the stitches into even gathers until the strip fits the bottom ring, leaving a slight overlap. Machine-stitch close to the running stitches to secure the gathers. Repeat this process for the top, using six strips measuring 12 inches long and 1 ½ inches wide joined to make two strips three times the circumference.

9 Glue the center line of the longer ruffle ½ inch above the bottom of the frame, overlapping the ends. Glue the shorter ruffle ¼ inch below the top ring.

10 At intervals of 1 inch pinch together the outside edges of the inside ruffle, top and bottom; secure with a drop of glue.

34

1 Start by binding the top and bottom rings (see Techniques, page 101).

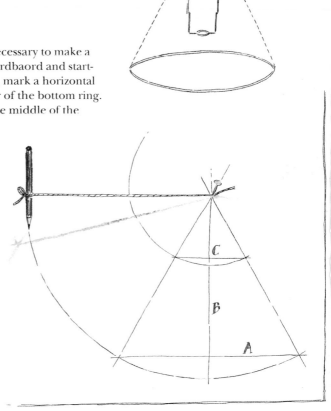

2 For a cone-shaped shade, it is necessary to make a pattern. Take a large sheet of thin cardbaord and starting in the bottom right-hand corner, mark a horizontal line A, equal to the 11-inch diameter of the bottom ring. Draw a vertical line B, up through the middle of the horizontal one and mark a point 6 inches, or the height of the shade, above the first one. Center a second horizontal line C through this point as long as the diameter of the top ring, which in this case is 4 inches. Draw the sides of the shade, continuing the lines upward until they meet.

To create the outline of the pattern, pin a length of string or ribbon to the tip of the triangle, and using a pencil attached to the end of the string, draw two arcs; start one at the top right-hand corner of the shade shape and the other at the bottom right-hand corner. The top and bottom arcs should be as long as the circumference of the top and bottom of the shade plus ½ inch overlap.

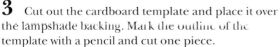

3 Cut out the cardboard template and place it over the lampshade backing. Mark the outline of the template with a pencil and cut one piece.

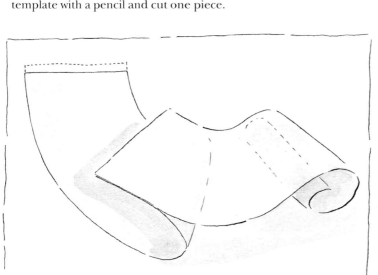

4 Position the backing over the wrong side of the fabric on the bias, making sure you have ⅜ yard of fabric left. Peel back 1 inch of the backing paper and stick the laminate firmly in place. Carefully pull back the backing paper from under the laminate, making sure the laminate adheres to the fabric smoothly with no creases. You may find it easier to pin the fabric securely in place before you start.

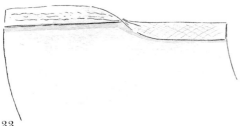

5 Cut out the silk fabric around the backing, adding an extra ½-inch seam allowance at one of the sides. Dribble a line of fabric glue along the wrong side of this seam allowance and stick it smoothly to the backing.

woven ribbons

Instead of using a panel of fabric, this novel shade is covered with a close basketweave of gingham ribbon. Here, only one pattern of ribbon is used but you can choose any sort of ribbon or combination of colors to create your woven shade. Adjust your measurements according to the width of the ribbons used and the size of the frame, and follow the simple weaving principle, finishing the top and bottom with a bright contrasting trim.

materials & equipment

rectangular frame with curved long sides and reversible top gimbal: 5 x 10½-inch bottom; 3 x 6½-inch top; with 10-in long curved sides and 4-in measurement across the middle, top and bottom

15 yards gingham ribbon, 1 inch wide

½-inch-wide binding tape

1½ yards contrasting bias binding, ½ inch wide

fabric glue

basic sewing kit (see page 98)

5 Starting at the top, weave the horizontal ribbons in and out of the vertical ones all around the shade. Pin the ends to the side strut and trim them back, leaving a ¼-inch seam allowance.

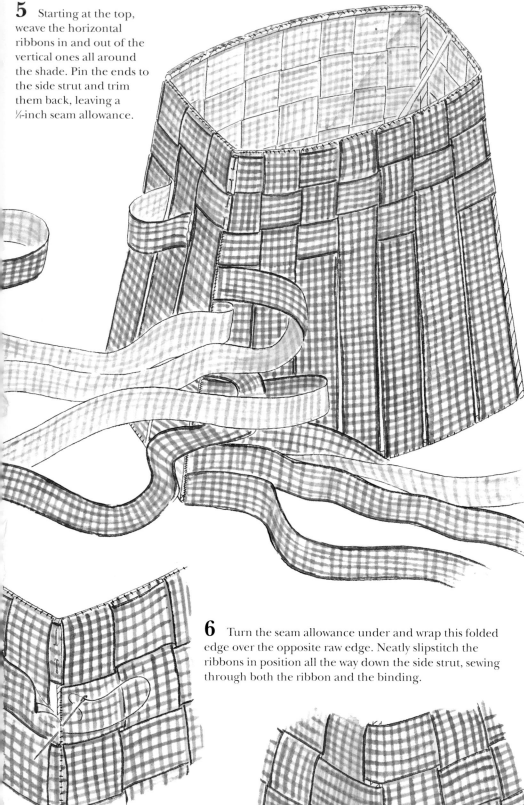

6 Turn the seam allowance under and wrap this folded edge over the opposite raw edge. Neatly slipstitch the ribbons in position all the way down the side strut, sewing through both the ribbon and the binding.

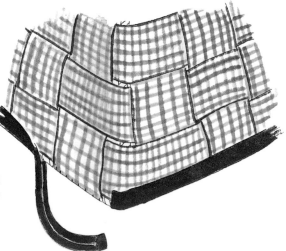

7 To hide the raw edges of the ribbon, cut out two strips of bias binding to fit the top and bottom, adding a ½-inch seam allowance. Glue the binding in position around the edges and turn under one end; overlap this end over the raw one to create a neat seam.

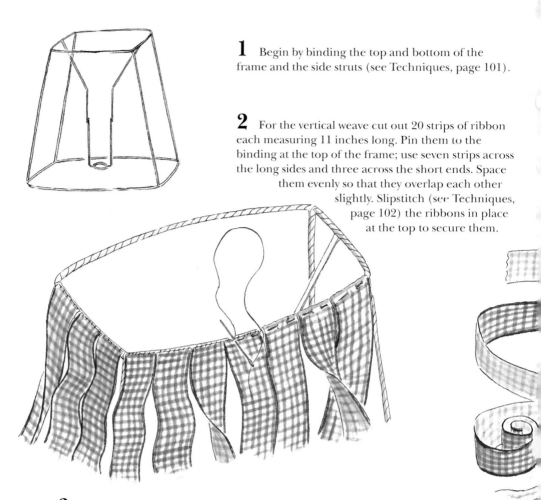

1 Begin by binding the top and bottom of the frame and the side struts (see Techniques, page 101).

2 For the vertical weave cut out 20 strips of ribbon each measuring 11 inches long. Pin them to the binding at the top of the frame; use seven strips across the long sides and three across the short ends. Space them evenly so that they overlap each other slightly. Slipstitch (see Techniques, page 102) the ribbons in place at the top to secure them.

3 Pull each ribbon down and pin to the bottom of the frame. As the bottom is wider than the top, the ribbons will be more spaced out at the base; make sure this spacing is even. Slipstitch the ribbons to the binding and trim the ends.

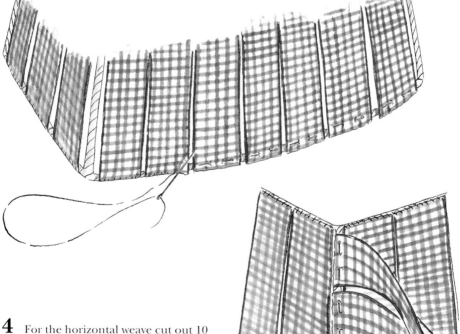

4 For the horizontal weave cut out 10 strips of ribbon each measuring 32 inches. Pin each length to one of the side struts, working from the top to the bottom and spacing them evenly. Slipstitch the ribbons in position.

tutu in voile

Because of the loose gathering of the slightly stiff organza material, the shade takes on the appearance of a ballerina's tutu, and the voile ribbon circling the top gives the whole design delicacy and movement. This pretty shade is surprisingly simple to make, consisting of a plain white lined frame sheathed in a translucent voile; gauze, lace or other sheer cloths would work just as well, and a different-colored lining would diffuse the light.

materials & equipment

cone-shaped frame with clip fitting and six side struts:
4-inch diameter top; 11-inch diameter bottom; 7-inch height

⅝ yard silk lining fabric, 45 inches wide

⅝ yard organza, 60 inches wide

½-inch-wide binding tape

1⅜ yards organza ribbon, 1½ inches wide

fabric marker

basic sewing kit (see page 98)

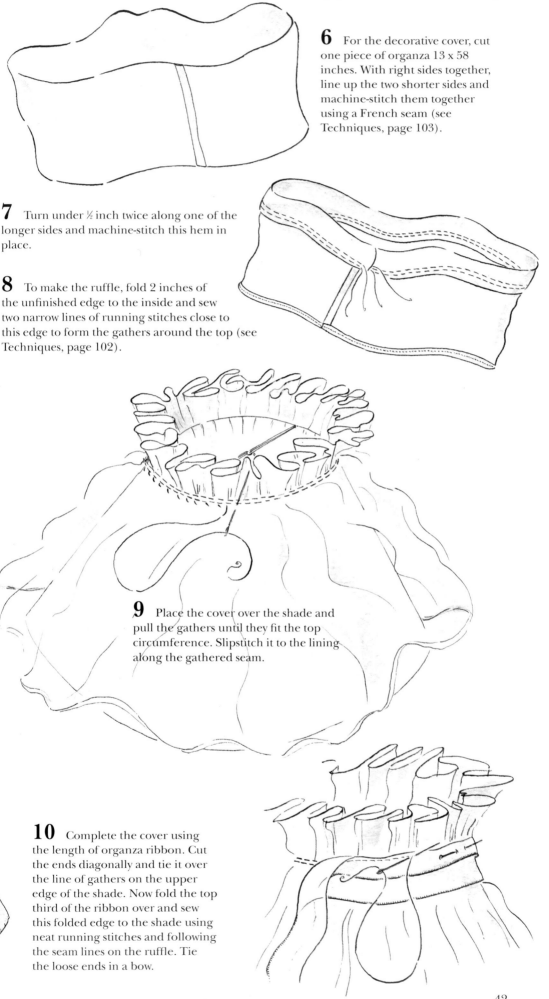

6 For the decorative cover, cut one piece of organza 13 x 58 inches. With right sides together, line up the two shorter sides and machine-stitch them together using a French seam (see Techniques, page 103).

7 Turn under ½ inch twice along one of the longer sides and machine-stitch this hem in place.

8 To make the ruffle, fold 2 inches of the unfinished edge to the inside and sew two narrow lines of running stitches close to this edge to form the gathers around the top (see Techniques, page 102).

9 Place the cover over the shade and pull the gathers until they fit the top circumference. Slipstitch it to the lining along the gathered seam.

10 Complete the cover using the length of organza ribbon. Cut the ends diagonally and tie it over the line of gathers on the upper edge of the shade. Now fold the top third of the ribbon over and sew this folded edge to the shade using neat running stitches and following the seam lines on the ruffle. Tie the loose ends in a bow.

1 Start by binding the rings and the side struts (see Techniques, page 101).

2 Measure and cut a piece of lining fabric 15 x 35½ inches. Use your fabric marker to mark six sections along the length, top, and bottom; the sections must be equal in length except for an additional ½-inch seam allowance at the ends. Next mark a line along the center of the length.

3 Line up this center line with the bottom ring of the frame and pin it to the binding, turning under and overlapping the side edges where they meet. Slip-stitch (see Techniques, page 102) the fabric to the bottom edge, taking the needle through both the fabric and the binding.

4 Taking the silk from the inside first, pull it up and over the top of the frame; match up and pin the six marked sections to the six side struts, making slits to fit the lining around the arms of the clip fitting. Pull the fabric together into small pleats between the struts and pin to the top frame. Hemstitch (see Techniques, page 102) to the top binding; trim.

5 Repeat this process for the silk outer covering, but turn under the raw edge around the top for a neat finish.

table lamps

This category of lamp covers an overwhelming variety to choose from. Styles include slender candlesticks topped with tiny shades; half shades ideal for setting at each end of a mantelpiece or on narrow shelving; heavy urn-like bases carrying sizable shades that may sit on a coffee or occasional table to provide pools of soft, atmospheric light; reading lights set upon a desk; or pretty dresser or bedside lights suitable for the bedroom.

left A white plaster base with a cone shade, laminated with a bright blue polka dot weave. *below from left* White dotted Swiss, finished with a ruffle; a generous Provençal cotton skirt, gathered with a bow; floral cotton, laminated onto a cone shape over a classical glass column base.

above A tall turned base, topped with a gathered shade in thin blue woven cotton. *right* A versatile brass table lamp, with maximum maneuverability, with a beautifully finished box-pleated shade.

above, left Pretty and practical: a tilt-top desk lamp with a collared shade is finished in a gathered double ruffle.

left, top to bottom A gathered cone with a difference – pale yellow silk is knife-pleated and finished in a blue binding, which is picked up by the matching two-toned deep fringes; striped fabric, neatly box pleated over an Empire shade, is finished in a strong complementary bias binding; a very elegant narrow tapered oval is a good shape to use when there is not much depth of space available.

above Polka-dotted voile, tightly gathered over this Empire shade, lets out maximum light; the top and bottom edges of this shade have been smartly finished with pinch-pleated silk and a contrasting color threaded through it.

below A traditional bouillotte tole lamp looks fresh with a pair of blue-and-white striped gathered shades.

box-pleated conical shade

Hiding an ordinary conical shade is a box-pleated cover made in warm red and yellow *toile de Jouy*. The skirt falls in loose folds, allowing the pattern of the fabric to remain visible. The bow is a pretty feature highlighting the waist of the shade and the ruffled effect of the box pleats at the top.

materials & equipment

*frame with six struts and reverse gimbal fitting: 5-inch diameter top;
10-inch diameter bottom; 7-inch height*

⅜ yard lining fabric, 45 inches wide

1¼ yards toile de Jouy fabric, 45 inches wide

½-inch-wide binding tape

basic sewing kit (see page 98)

6 For the loose outer shade, cut out a panel of *toile de Jouy*, 12½ x 60 inches, joining pieces and matching patterns as necessary. Fold the panel in half widthwise, right sides facing, and machine-stitch the short ends with a ⅜-inch seam allowance. To finish the seam allowance, turn each side under by ¼-inch and machine-stitch down, making sure you do not sew through to the main fabric.

7 Fold in a double ¼-inch hem along the bottom edge of the circle of fabric; pin, baste, and machine-stitch in position. Next fold in the top edge of the fabric to the wrong side by 2½ inch and baste in place.

8 Make a series of box pleats around the top by folding the material into itself; there should be 12 pleats, each with two ⅜-inch sides and a 1½-inch front panel. Pin the pleats and check the fit on the shade, making small adjustments where necessary. Baste and machine-stitch the pleats in place 2 inches below the top folded edge.

9 Slip the cover over the frame and sew a line of running stitches (see Techniques, page 102) through all layers, just under the top ring and following the stitches made in step 8.

10 To make the bow, cut out a strip of *toile de Jouy*, measuring 2½ x 55 inches. If necessary, join strips together matching the pattern. Fold in half lengthwise with right sides facing and cut the short ends at a slight angle. Machine-stitch along the long edge and one of the shorter ones with a ¼-inch seam allowance.

11 Use a knitting needle or a safely pin to push the fabric right side out through the open end. Tuck the raw ends to the inside and neatly sew the opening closed. Tie in a bow around the top of the frame.

1 Start by binding the top and bottom rings of the frame and the side struts with binding tape (see Techniques, page 101).

2 Cut out two pieces of lining fabric, 8 x 32½ inches. Mark six equal sections on the long edges top and bottom with small snips but leave an extra ½-inch seam allowance at the two short ends.

3 Pin one piece of lining fabric to the outside of the frame along the bottom, lining up the marks with the struts. Where the fabric meets, fold back the seam allowance on one end and place it so that it overlaps the raw edge on the other side. Pull the fabric up over the frame and start by pinning the marks to the struts, then pin small, even pleats between the marks. Hemstitch (see Techniques, page 102) the lining in place and trim.

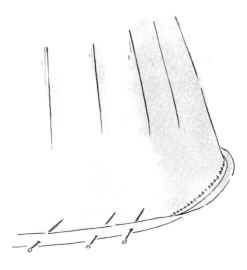

4 Now pin the second piece of lining fabric to the inside of the frame, making two small slits at the top to accommodate the gimbal arms. Line up and pin the fabric as in step 3, but at the top and bottom, fold under the edge by ¼ inch, positioning it over the existing raw edge for a neat finish. Hemstitch top and bottom and trim.

5 To finish the gimbal arms, cut out two strips of lining fabric 1½ x 2¾ inches. Fold both the long edges to the middle and wrap each strip under the gimbal arm. Tuck under the raw edge, and pin and neatly hand sew to the top of the frame.

smocked patterned shade

A pretty blue Provençal skirt with a smocked top is slipped over a plain lined shade; the elasticized top means that the cover stays firmly in place. Choose any motif pattern as an alternative. The great thing about this practical design is that it can be removed easily to shake the dust off or be washed.

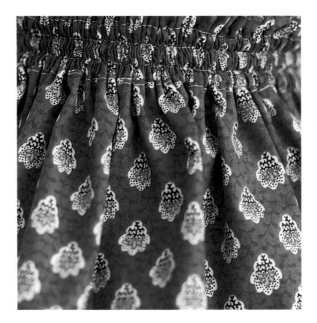

materials & equipment

frame with eight side struts and duplex fitting: 6½-inch diameter top; 10-inch diameter bottom; 7-inch height, including 1½-inch collar

1⅞ yards lining fabric, 45 inches wide

⅝ yard Provençal cotton, 60 inches wide

½-inch-wide binding tape

1¾ yards elastic, ¼-inch wide

basic sewing kit (see page 98)

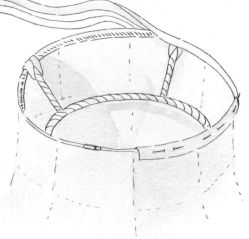

7 To hide the raw edges cut a strip of lining fabric 33 x 1 in for the bottom and 22 x 1 inches for the top. On both strips fold the long edges to the middle and press. Pin, then slipstitch (see Techniques, page 102) the strips in place along both folded edges, tucking under the raw ends for a neat finish.

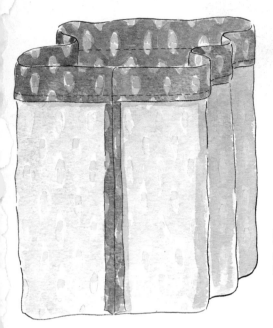

8 For the smocked skirt cut a piece of Provençal cotton 18 x 51 inches. Fold it in half, matching the short ends, right sides facing, and pin and machine-stitch together, using a ½-inch seam allowance. Press open the seam.

9 With the tube of fabric wrong side out, fold down the top edge by 2½ inches and pin and baste it in place.

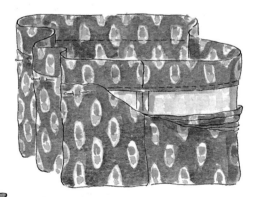

10 Now turn the bottom edge up ¼ inch and press, then fold the whole lower half of the tube up; overlap the bottom folded edge and the basted raw edge by ¼ inch. Pin and machine-stitch the overlap joining all layers together.

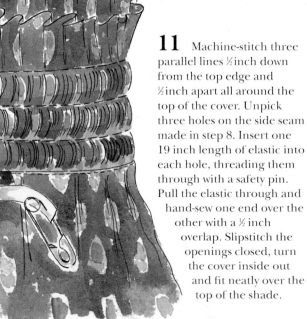

11 Machine-stitch three parallel lines ½ inch down from the top edge and ½ inch apart all around the top of the cover. Unpick three holes on the side seam made in step 8. Insert one 19 inch length of elastic into each hole, threading them through with a safety pin. Pull the elastic through and hand-sew one end over the other with a ½ inch overlap. Slipstitch the openings closed, turn the cover inside out and fit neatly over the top of the shade.

1 | Start by binding all parts of the frame with binding tape (see Techniques, page 101).

2 | Cut four pieces of lining fabric, 8 x 17 inches. Pin one to half of the outside of the frame, starting in the middle of the top and bottom rings, then at the sides and corners, and continue pinning at opposite sides, keeping the fabric tight. Mark the outline of the pins with a pencil before removing the lining from the frame. Using this as a template, cut three more pieces of lining fabric, adding a 1-inch seam allowance around the pencil outlines.

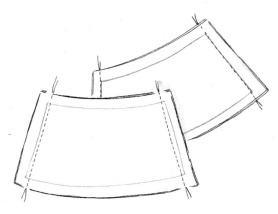

3 | For the outer casing, machine-stitch two panels of lining fabric together down the sides, right sides facing, and following the pencil lines exactly. Repeat for the inner casing, but reduce the width between the pencil markings by ⅛ inch at each side for a tight fit.

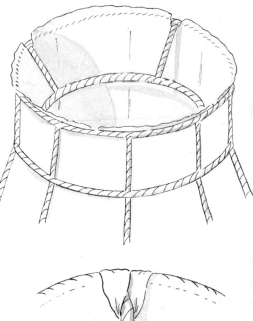

4 | Slip the inner casing inside the frame with the wrong side facing out. Line up the side seams with two opposite struts, and pin into position around the top and bottom, pulling the fabric tight. Make four small snips at the top to fit the lining around the arms. Hemstitch (see Techniques, page 102) the lining to the binding around the top and bottom of the frame and trim.

5 | Slip the outer lining casing over the top of the shade, aligning the seams with those on the inner casing. Pin and hemstitch in place, top and botttom.

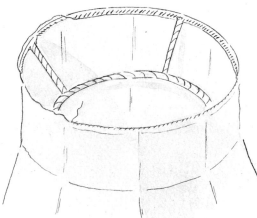

6 | Cut out four strips of lining fabric 1 x 2½ inches. Fold both long edges to the middle and wrap a strip under each arm of the duplex fitting. Hand-sew to the frame top and trim.

covered shade

This cloche hat shade is made from a pink silk taffeta and trimmed with cream silk and a handmade rosette at the top. The heavily gathered effect all around the shade is achieved by a series of narrow, even knife pleats at the top, stretching down to meet the tightly gathered bottom circumference. Because the shade is covered over the top it is vital to use a very low-watt bulb positioned well below the covering, to minimize the risk of scorching.

materials & equipment

frame with six side struts, six top struts and reverse gimbal fitting: 9½-inch diameter bottom; 6-inch diameter top; 1½-inch diameter center ring; 5½-inch height

1⅛ yards pink silk taffeta, 45 inches wide

⅜ yard lining fabric, 45 inches wide

⅜ yard cream silk, 45 inches wide

basic sewing kit (see page 98)

scalloped crown

This unusual shade is made from a single piece of lilac and white checked cotton stiffened with iron-on interfacing to allow it to stand upright yet remain loosely attached to the frame. The scallops are made in a curve along the bottom edge so the brim is deeper at the front and gradually slopes down as it meets the seam at the back. If the mathematics of the scallops deters you, simply straighten the top edge and have a plain smoothly curving brim.

materials & equipment

frame with four struts and a base fitting: 6-inch diameter bottom ring; 3-inch diameter top ring; 12-inch height

¼ yard lilac and white checked reversible cotton, 45 inches wide

⅛ yard medium-weight iron-on interfacing

½-inch-wide binding tape

20-inch square cardboard for template

6 With the fabric wrong side up once again, work a narrow zigzag along the curved edges of the bottom scallops using a contrasting burgundy thread. This will strengthen, and decorate the raw edges.

7 Flip the fabric to the right side again and work the same zigzag along the curved edges of the top scallops and down the right-hand side.

8 Turn up the lower portion of the shade by making a fold along the lower line of interfacing. Run a line of fabric adhesive down the outside edge of the plain side and press it onto the inside of the opposite edge, thus forming a hat shape.

9 Slip the shade over the frame. To prevent the loose-fitting shade from slipping off the frame, make tiny stab stitches at three points spaced around the top and bottom rings of the frame, taking the needle through both the fabric and the binding.

1 Bind the entire frame (see Techniques, page 101).

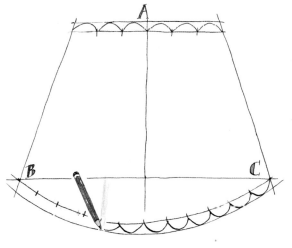

2 For the template, draw a vertical line measuring 12 inches, and a horizontal one across its base with 10 inches on each side of the vertical. At the top of the vertical line draw another horizontal line extending for 6 inches on each side. Join the sides. At point A, pin a piece of string with a pencil attached and draw an arc from B to C. Draw a second arc 1 inches below the first one. Place a piece of string along the first arc, and measure and mark it into twelve equal sections. Carefully draw twelve scallops between the marks with the top of each scallop meeting the outer arc. For the scallops along the top, divide the top line into six equal sections, then draw a horizontal line 1 inch above it; use the marks to draw six scallops as before.

3 Use the template to cut out the pattern with the check fabric on the bias (see Techniques, page 103). Mark the widest horizontal line across the fabric very lightly with a pencil on both sides.

4 With the fabric wrong side up, cut a piece of iron-on interfacing slightly larger all around than the upper portion of the pattern, aligning a straight edge of interfacing along the pencil line. Iron on the interfacing and trim off the excess around the sides and top edge.

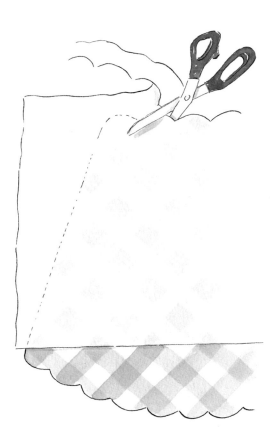

5 Turn the fabric over so it is right side up and cut a piece of iron-on interfacing slightly larger all around than the portion below the line. Align a straight edge of interfacing ½ inch below the line. Iron on the interfacing and trim away the excess around the sides and bottom scalloped edge.

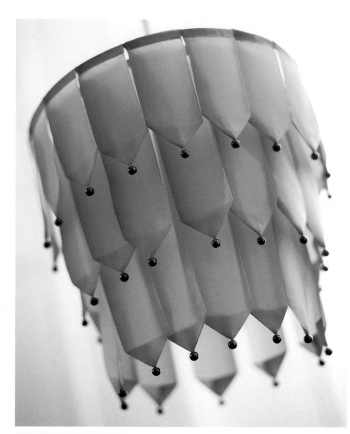

clockwise from top Layered taffeta ribbons finished with beads; wall sconces in velvet and pale checked cotton; a period brass wall bracket with a gathered cotton shade; yellow laminated burlap on a pendant drum shade; metal eyelets with rings attach a loose shade to a circular frame; pretty printed floaty voile is gathered tightly on a collared pendant.

Thin yellow cotton was dipped in fabric stiffener and then draped over a paneled shade. The molded shape was then finished with a satin tassel.

This fun harlequin chandelier was knitted from fine yellow silk and draped over a ring frame. Gilt coins catch the light and keep the shade in shape.

A tightly knitted pagoda-shaped pendant, stretched over a series of ring frames, makes a most effective and clever overhead light fixture.

wall and ceiling lamps

Ceiling lights tend to operate as main sources of light, often illuminating a whole room. Although they should be capable of casting plenty of light, they should also be a decorative feature and draw the eye up. Wall lights come as uplights, bracket lights, and sconces, and are useful for throwing light onto surrounding surfaces that reflect back into the room.

above Thin gray and cream striped voile is tightly gathered to form a dense cover on a circular wall shield, which curves gently to hide the bulb from view on each side. A flame retardant lining is used to prevent scorching.
left A wall sconce throws light in a wide arc up to the ceiling and creates a wonderfully subtle effect. This one is laminated with rich yellow crushed velvet and edged with a laced leather thong.

linen
loose cover

An ornate wall sconce is topped with a piece of the palest apricot linen no bigger than a pocket handkerchief. The soft-hued fabric sits loosely on a cardboard shade and looks as if it has just floated down and settled in place, creating a gentle pool of background light for a relaxed atmosphere.

materials & equipment

cardboard undershade with bulb fitting: 3-inch diameter top; 7-inch diameter bottom; 5 ¼-inch height

⅝ yard apricot linen, 45 inches wide

pattern paper

compass or pencil, thumbtack and string

basic sewing kit (see page 98)

5 Turn the fabric right side up and lay it flat. Mark the positions of three small box pleats around the inner circle; these points and the opening should be positioned to mark the four quarters of the circle.

6 At the three marked points, make a box pleat by folding the fabric into itself on two sides – both tucks and the part forming the back of the pleat should each measure ¼ inch. Pin and baste in place. The inner circle should now have a 10-inch circumference.

7 Cut a strip of linen on the bias, 1½ x 27 inches. With right sides together, center the strip along the main fabric, and pin and baste it ¼ inch below the top raw edge. Machine-stitch the strip in place ¼ inch from the edge, leaving two 8 ½ inch tails.

8 Turn the long raw edge of the strip over the top raw edge of the main fabric and fold under ¼ inch. Pin and slipstitch (see Techniques, page 102) it to the wrong side, hiding the row of machine stitches.

9 To finish the ends fold in the raw edges by ¼ inch and slipstitch the opening (as in step 8) to a neat close. Press the cover.

10 Wrap the cover around the undershade and tie the ends in a bow to hold it in place.

1 Start by making a template for the cover using a piece of paper 18 inches square. To create the outline of the pattern, pin a length of string or tape to the center of the paper and using a pencil attached to the end of the string, draw a circle with an 8 inch radius, then adjust the string to draw a smaller circle with a 1⅜-inch radius in the middle of the outer one. Cut out the outer circle, followed by the inner circle.

2 Pin the template onto the linen fabric and cut one piece, then cut a straight line between the outer and inner circumferences.

3 Turn under and pin a double ⅛-inch fold all round the outer circumference. Hemstitch (see Techniques page 102) the fold in place on the wrong side.

4 Next turn under and pin a double ⅛-inch fold along both the straight edges, making a neat right-angle fold at the corners, over the bottom hem. Hemstitch the folds in place and press.

gingham in gathers

For a lampshade like this miniature square, a small-scale pattern such as gingham is ideal. To give the tiny shade a little more impact, the gingham has been very tightly gathered all around the top and bottom, and a matching braid has been attached to finish the edges and add a decorative touch.

materials & equipment

square frame with four side struts and clip fitting: 3½-inch square top; 5-inch square bottom; 4-inch height

⅝ yard blue and white gingham, 45 inches wide

⅝ yard white silk lampshade lining, 45 inches wide

½-inch-wide binding tape

1¼ yards decorative braid

fabric glue

basic sewing kit (see page 98)

5 To line the shade, cut one piece of silk lining measuring 5½ x 21 inches. Mark into four sections top and bottom, adding a ½-inch seam allowance at the ends. Sew two narrow lines of running stitches along the top to form gathers as in step 2. Then pin the lining to the inside of the shade top and bottom, lining up the sections with the four struts. Pull the raw edges over the frame, making small slits in the top to fit around the bulb clip.

6 Fold the raw edges under ¼ inch; pin and hemstitch in place. Finish the side seams in the same way as for the gingham cover.

7 Cut the decorative braid to fit the top and bottom, adding an extra ½-inch overlap. Glue it in place with fabric glue, turning under one of the raw ends for neat finish.

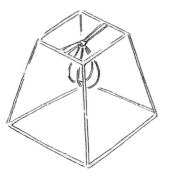

1 Bind the frame around the top and bottom and down the side struts (see Techniques, page 101).

2 Cut out one piece of main fabric 5 x 40 inches and mark it into quarters by making small snips no deeper than ¼ inches at the top and bottom. Sew two narrow lines of running stitches along the top and bottom and pull gently to form gathers. When gathered, the top edge should be 14 inches long and the bottom edge, 20 inches long.

3 Attach the fabric to the frame by first matching the quarter sections with the four corners of the frame top and bottom. Pin the corners first and then pin around the sides. Where the fabric meets, turn under ¼ inch on one edge and place it ¼ inch over the opposite one.

4 Hemstitch the fabric in place (see Techniques, page 102) and trim the edges.

chandelier candle shades

Six miniature cones with pretty scalloped edges are made from laminated yellow gingham; here, the tiny checks mean there is an even distribution of light through the shade. The shades are quick and easy to make using a template and each one sits neatly on a bulb clip on each arm of a chandelier.

materials & equipment

2-inch diameter bulb clip: 2-inch diameter top;
5-inch diameter bottom; 4-inch height

7 x 14 inches yellow cotton gingham for each shade

7 x 14 inches self-adhesive backing for each shade

clothespins

basic sewing kit (see page 98)

3 Peel the protective coating away from the adhesive backing and press the exposed sticky surface to the wrong side of the fabric. Smooth out any air bubbles or crinkles from the center out. Press firmly together.

4 Using the cardboard made in step 1, draw around the edges of the pattern onto the laminated back of the fabric with a pencil, then cut out.

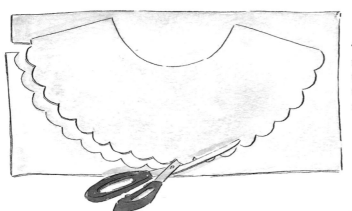

5 Run a line of glue down the straight inside edge and press to the front of the side with the overlap. Use two clothespins to hold the edges firmly together until the glue is completely dry.

6 Remove the clothespins when the glue is dry and simply slip the shade over the top of a "candle" bulb clip.

7 Repeat this process for each shade on the chandelier. They are so simple to make and assemble, that you can make several sets in different colors to change the mood of a room or introduce a new theme.

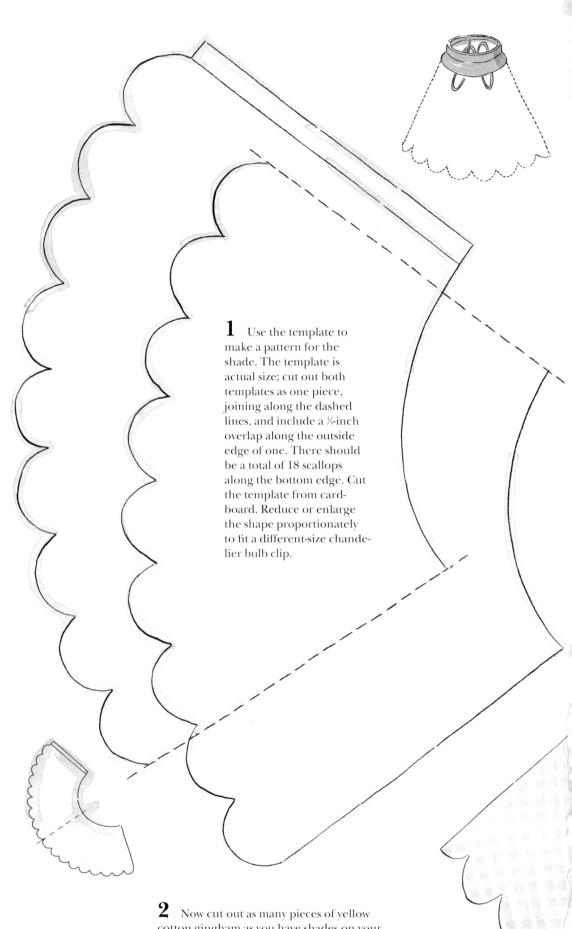

1 Use the template to make a pattern for the shade. The template is actual size; cut out both templates as one piece, joining along the dashed lines, and include a ¼-inch overlap along the outside edge of one. There should be a total of 18 scallops along the bottom edge. Cut the template from card-board. Reduce or enlarge the shape proportionately to fit a different-size chandelier bulb clip.

2 Now cut out as many pieces of yellow cotton gingham as you have shades on your chandelier, each one measuring 7 x 14 inches. Repeat this process for the self-adhesive backing.

two-tiered hanging lamp

This exquisite ceiling lamp is perfect for hanging over a kitchen or dining room table. It is a Swedish design and consists of a pretty cotton print tailored around a cone-shaped frame and an outer ring covered by a deep gathered ruffle that hangs down, giving an original two-tiered effect.

materials & equipment

frame with six side struts and brass ceiling gimbal mechanism: 3-inch diameter top; 14-inch diameter bottom; 9-inch height; four 3-inch arms join 17-inch diameter outer bottom ring

¾ yard lining fabric, 45 inches wide

1⅜ yards red and white cotton print, 60 inches wide

basic sewing kit (see page 98)

7 To finish the bottom of the inner ring (the top ring will be covered by a brass fitting), cut a strip of main fabric 1½ x 43 inches. Fold both long edges to the wrong side by ¼ inch and press. Pin and slipstitch (see Techniques, page 102) in place around the upper and lower edges of the binding, tucking in the ends to hide the raw edges. Make tiny slits in the strip to fit the arms.

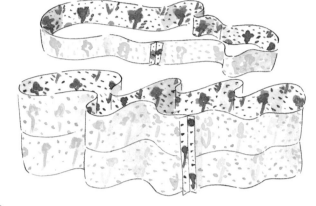

8 For the outer ruffle cut out one panel of the main fabric measuring 14 x 78 inches and a strip, 2 inches wide and as long as the circumference of the outer ring, plus an extra 1 inch for the seam allowance; join pieces and match patterns as necessary. With right sides facing, machine-stitch the short ends together on each piece using a ½-inch seam allowance.

9 Fold the main fabric in half, matching raw edges with wrong sides facing, and sew two narrow lines of running stitches ½ inch from the top raw edge. Pull the threads into even gathers to fit the circumference of the outer ring. Using a ½-inch seam allowance, pin and machine-stitch the fabric to the strip, right sides facing and matching raw edges.

10 Place the ruffle around the outer ring, wrapping the wrong side of the strip over the frame. Tuck under the raw edge on the strip, make slits to fit the arms, and pin and slipstitch it to the underside of the bound frame.

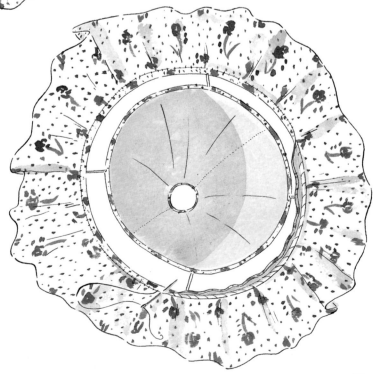

1 Bind the top and both the inner and outer bottom rings of the frame with binding tape (see Techniques, page 101).

2 Cut two pieces of lining fabric, 11 x 23 inches. Pin one piece to half of the frame on the outside, top and bottom, adjusting the pins as you pull the fabric tight. Mark the outline of the pins with a pencil to show the seamlines, before removing them.

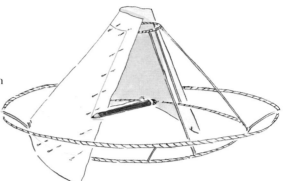

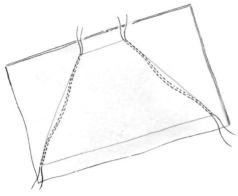

3 Pin the second piece of lining to the pencil-marked one, right sides facing. Baste along the pencil lines at the side, but reduce the width at the "waist" by ¼ inch on each side for a tight fit. Machine-stitch two narrow lines down both curved edges, following the basting stitches, and trim the excess fabric.

4 Slip the lining casing inside the frame with the seam allowances facing out and the seams aligned with side struts. Pin to the top and bottom rings of the frame so the fabric is tight. Hemstitch (see Techniques, page 102) to the binding tape and trim.

5 Cut out a panel of main fabric 60 x 11 inches, joining pieces together and matching patterns as necessary. Mark into six equal sections top and bottom with small snips, leaving a ½-inch seam allowance at each short end.

6 Begin by pinning the marks to the six side struts top and bottom, turning in and overlapping one raw end ½ inch over the other. Pin a series of even knife pleats between the marks along the top, until the fabric fits the ring exactly. Fan the pleats out evenly and pin around the bottom edge. Hemstitch the top and bottom of the cover and trim.

striped wall shield

This tiny half-shade is designed to shield a bulb on a wall sconce. The unusual shape is ideal for elaborate and ornate sconces. The striped silk taffeta is stretched very tightly around the frame, and the same stripe is cut on the bias to trim the edges. The project is entirely hand-stitched.

materials & equipment

half-cylinder frame with bulb clip fitting: 6¼-inches wide;
5-inch height at center; 4¼-inch height at sides

¼ yard striped silk taffeta, 45 inches wide

⅛ yard lining fabric, 45 inches wide

basic sewing kit (see page 98)

6 To hide the seams where the arms of the bulb clip meet the top of the frame, cut out two strips of lining 1 x 2 inches. Fold the long edges of each strip to the center and press. Wrap a strip around each end, then pin and hand-sew the ends of the strip to the frame. Trim away the excess.

7 Cut a strip of silk taffeta on the bias (see Techniques, page 103) so that the stripes run diagonally, 1 x 21¼ inches. Fold in ¼ inch along both long edges and press flat.

8 Pin the bias binding around the perimeter of the frame to hide the raw edges, positioning the upper edge along the top. Start and end in a corner, turning under one raw edge to overlap the other; form neat tucks at the remaining corners where the fabric bunches.

9 Slipstitch in place (see Techniques, page 102), along both folded edges so that the stitches are almost invisible.

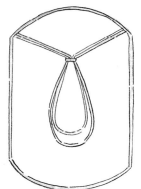

1. Start by binding all round the frame with binding tape (see Techniques, page 101).

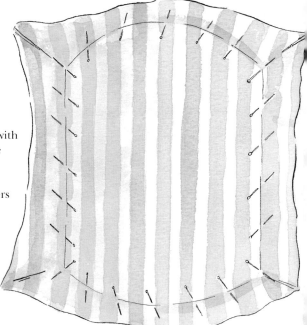

2 Cut a piece of silk taffeta 7 x 8 inches with the stripes running vertically. Pin the piece around the edge of the front of the frame, pinning first in the center at the top and bottom and on the sides, then at the corners and then at opposite sides around the frame, pulling the fabric tight.

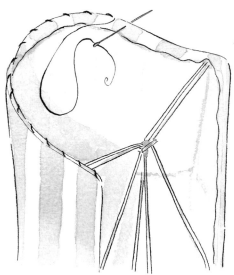

3 Hemstitch (see Techniques, page 102) to the binding all around the frame and trim.

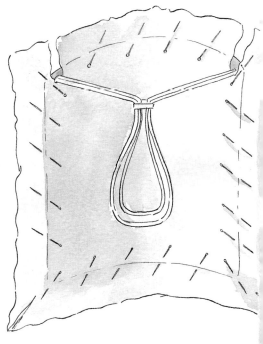

4 Next cut out a 7 x 8 inch piece of lining. Pin it around the edge of the reverse side of the frame in the same way as for the silk taffeta, overlapping the raw edge of the silk taffeta. Cut slits to fit the fabric around the arms of the bulb clip.

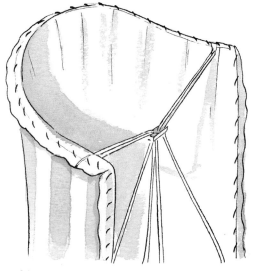

5 Once the pins are in position and the lining is really tight, hemstitch the lining to the binding all round the inside of the frame. Trim away the excess fabric.

floor lamps

By their nature, floor lamps tend to be more prominent than their counterparts found on walls, tables, and mantelpieces or shelves. Because they are free-standing and relatively tall, whether a traditional standing lamp or a lower gooseneck reading light, they need a shade in keeping with the height and shape of the stand.

above, from left A large boxed Empire shade looks handsome on a huge column base: a smaller shade would be dwarfed by such an impressive base. A modern metal base supports a more traditional box-pleated Empire shade made from a striped cotton – the wide openings at the top and base of the shade allow plenty of light to shine out. A tall narrow shape is ideal for a room where a floor lamp is the best solution, but space is limited; this cone is covered in crushed silk and sits on a simple metal pole. This cream silk square banded shade is gently waisted for an elegant feel.

right, from left A bicolored silk with wide stripes is cut out on the bias and simply laminated onto a conical shade. A filmy white fabric skirted shade sits atop a thin tripod base by Philip Starck. A pale aqua *toile de Jouy* fabric, knife pleated and finished with a gathered ruffle, covers the shade on a swing-armed standing lamp. A huge carved wooden base needs a proportionately large shade – this one is octagonal and covered in a pale check neatly mitered at the seams. Tall and elegant, this cone-topped stand with a three-pronged base would fit well into a modern setting.

stripes around a drum

A drum is a traditional shape for floor lamps, and the open top and bottom throw out plenty of light. Here the shade is simply a cylinder of laminated striped fabric. The formal stripes and stiff surface have been softened with ready-made double ball fringe.

materials & equipment

16-inch diameter plain wire ring

16-inch diameter gimbal wire ring

⅝ yard striped cotton, 45 inches wide

½-inch-wide binding tape

1½ yards single ball fringe

1½ yards double ball fringe

1¾ yards self-adhesive lampshade backing, 45 inches wide

fabric glue

clothespins

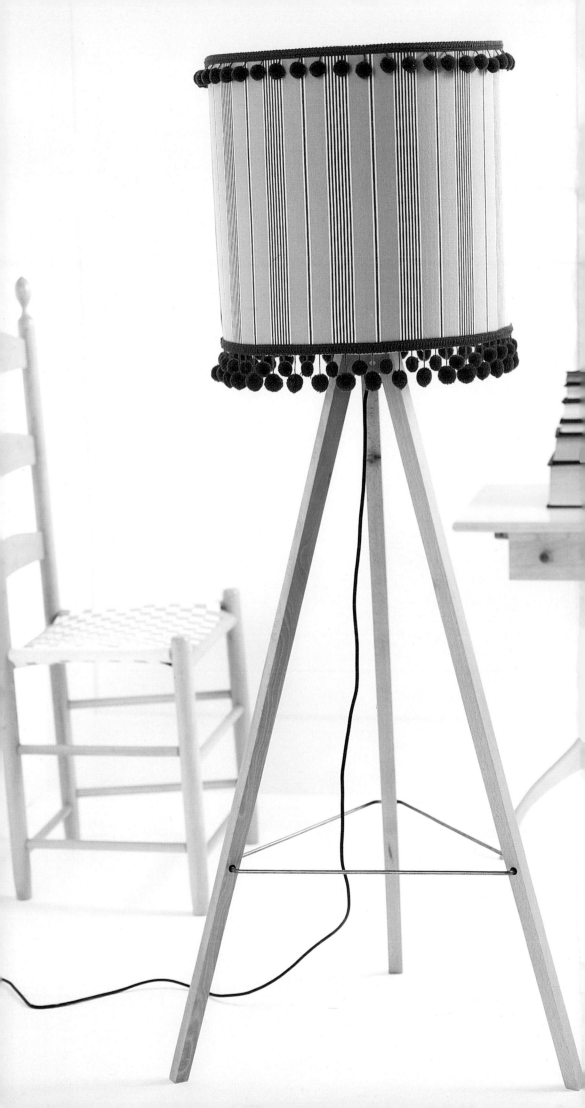

6 Seal up the side by squeezing a line of fabric adhesive down the overlap on the inside and sticking it to the opposite edge of the shade.

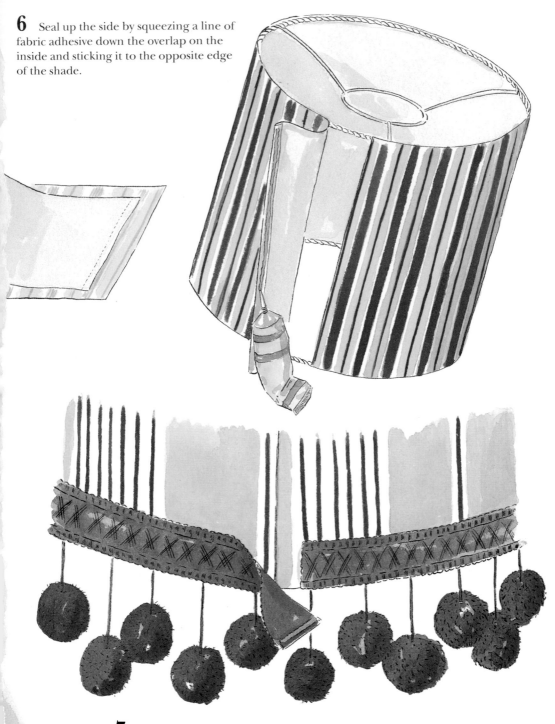

7 To trim, cut two 50½-inch lengths from each bobble fringe. Apply the fabric glue to the wrong side of each strip and the top and bottom outside edges of the shade. Starting at the seam, attach the strips to the drum, gluing the single row of bobbles to the top and the double row to the bottom. Where the two ends meet, turn in one raw edge and glue it over the other for a neat finish.

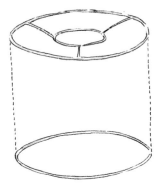

1   Start by binding both wire frames around the circumference (see Techniques, page 101).

2   Mark a rectangle on the backing paper measuring 16 x 50½ inches which allows for a ½-inch overlap at one of the shorter sides. Carefully cut out the shape.

3   Position the backing over the wrong side of the cotton fabric and gradually pull the protective sheet away, smoothing the two surfaces together.

4   Cut the fabric out around the backing, leaving an extra ¼ inch at one of the short ends. Fold this strip of material toward the backing and glue it down.

5   Clip the laminated fabric around the rings, top and bottom, pulling it tight as you go to check the fit. Remove the clothespins on one half to release a section of the cover. Apply a thin line of glue to the outside edges of the exposed rings and to the top and bottom inside edges of the loose section of the cover. Roll the cover back into position, lining up and pressing together the glued sections. Replace the clothespins around these edges while the glue sets. Repeat on the other side.

leather-stitched chimney

Vivid blue canvas is laminated to stiffen it and then cut and rolled into a tall cone or chimney shape. Because of the lamination, the fabric can be punched with holes so that a black leather thong can be threaded through it to secure the sides, creating an unusual fastening and trim.

material & equipment

4-inch diameter plain wire ring

10-inch diameter base fitting gimbal

1¼ yards blue canvas, 45 inches wide

½-inch-wide black binding tape

3½ yards leather thong

30-inch square thin cardboard

1¼ yards self-adhesive lampshade backing, 45 inches wide

multipurpose glue and clothespins

six-way hole punch

7 Now punch holes through the pencil marks using a six-way punch.

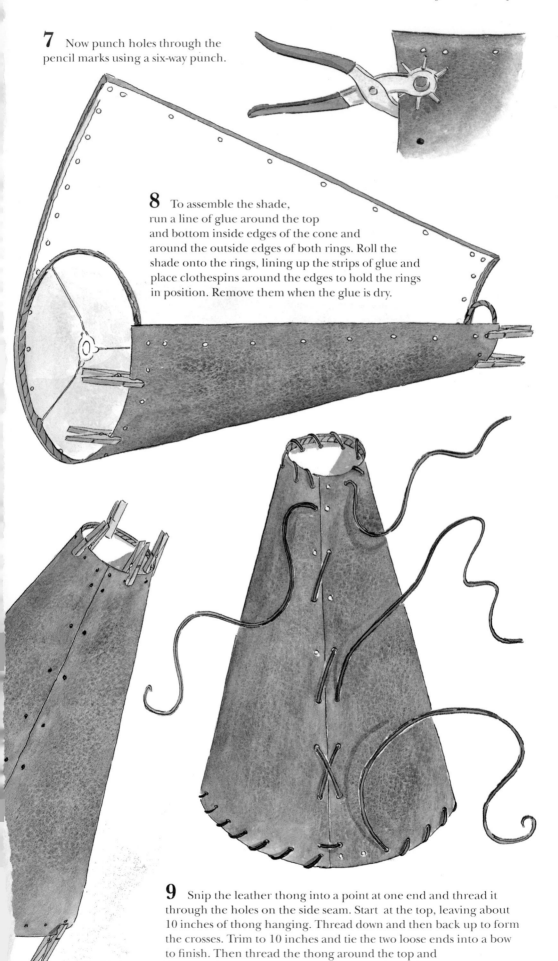

8 To assemble the shade, run a line of glue around the top and bottom inside edges of the cone and around the outside edges of both rings. Roll the shade onto the rings, lining up the strips of glue and place clothespins around the edges to hold the rings in position. Remove them when the glue is dry.

9 Snip the leather thong into a point at one end and thread it through the holes on the side seam. Start at the top, leaving about 10 inches of thong hanging. Thread down and then back up to form the crosses. Trim to 10 inches and tie the two loose ends into a bow to finish. Then thread the thong around the top and bottom edges, overlapping the rim. Knot the ends to secure.

1 First bind the smaller ring and the outside edge and struts of the base gimbal ring (see Techniques, page 101).

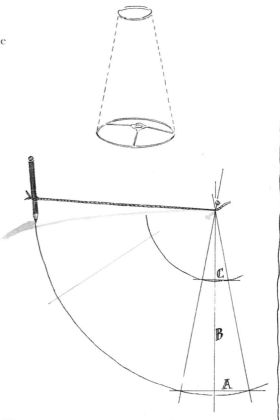

2 Take the cardboard and starting in the bottom right-hand corner, mark a horizontal line equal to the 10-inch diameter of the bottom ring (A). Draw a vertical line upward through the middle of the horizontal one and mark a point 4 inches, equal to the height of the shade, above the first one (B). Center a second horizontal line through this point 4 inches long, or equal to the diameter of the top ring (C). Draw in the sides of the shade, continuing the lines up until they meet.

   To create the outline of the pattern, pin a length of string to the tip of the triangle, and using a pencil attached to the end of the string, draw two arcs; start one at the top right-hand corner of the shade shape and the other at the bottom right-hand corner. The arcs should be as long as the circumference of the top and bottom of the shade plus ½-inch overlap.

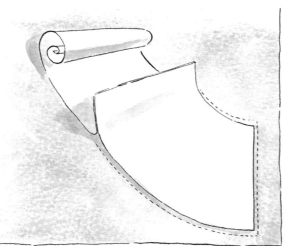

3 Cut out the template and place it over the lampshade backing. Mark the outline of the template and cut out one piece.

4 Position the backing over the wrong side of the fabric on the bias, and glue the two together by peeling back the protective sheet.

5 Cut out the fabric around the backing, adding an extra ½-inch overlap all the way around, cutting a triangle of fabric away at each corner to reduce the bulk. Drizzle a line of glue along the wrong side of this overlap, fold it over, and stick it to the backing.

6 Check the fit of the shade around the rings by cliping it in place. Mark the exact position of the overlap. Work out where the holes along the top and bottom edges and down the side seam should go, and mark them, too. The holes around the top and bottom should be about 1 inch apart. Remove the clothespins.

pleated
cone with collar

This frame has a distinctive profile, characterized by its elegant collar
at the top. The design contributes to the stylish look of a
lampshade made in formal pleats, which are pulled in at the neck by a
decorative binding and emphasized by the cream and
olive striped taffeta.

materials & equipment

*frame with six struts and drop pendant fitting: 6-inch diameter top;
10-inch diameter bottom; 8-inch height including
1¼-inch collar*

⅜ yard lining fabric, 45 inches wide

1¼ yards narrow striped taffeta, 45 inches wide

½-in-wide binding tape

fabric glue

basic sewing kit (see page 98)

6 Hemstitch top and bottom pleats in place and trim.

7 Cut a strip of taffeta 1½ x 20½ inches on the bias. Match the stripes and machine-stitch the ends, right sides together with a diagonal seam, using a ½-inch seam allowance.

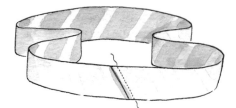

8 Fold in both raw edges by ½ inch and press. Slip the binding over the top of the frame to rest on the neck and secure with a few dabs of glue on the underside.

9 To trim the top, cut a strip of taffeta 1½ x 20½ inches on the bias, and join as above. Fold in one raw edge by ½ inch and press. Place the right side of the binding against the lining on the inside, with the raw edge positioned along the top of the frame; pin and then hemstitch the raw edge all the way around.

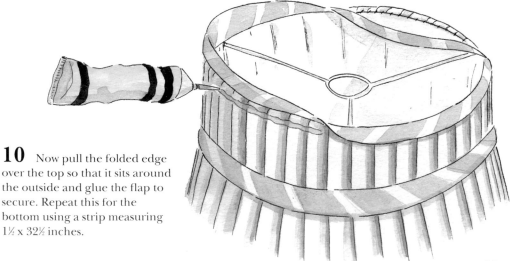

10 Now pull the folded edge over the top so that it sits around the outside and glue the flap to secure. Repeat this for the bottom using a strip measuring 1½ x 32½ inches.

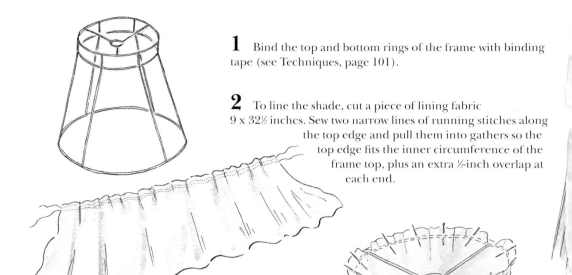

1 Bind the top and bottom rings of the frame with binding tape (see Techniques, page 101).

2 To line the shade, cut a piece of lining fabric 9 x 32½ inches. Sew two narrow lines of running stitches along the top edge and pull them into gathers so the top edge fits the inner circumference of the frame top, plus an extra ½-inch overlap at each end.

3 Pin the lining evenly inside the top ring, making three small snips to accommodate the pendant arms. Then turn in one raw edge by ½ inch to overlap the other and pin the bottom edge in place. Hemstitch (see Techniques page 102) to secure the lining top and bottom, and trim.

4 Cut two panels of striped taffeta measuring 9 x 45 inches. Each panel must be pleated to fit half the circumference of the shade with a ½-inch overlap at each short end. Pleat the top edge first where the pleats are tighter, and begin each one on the edge of a stripe; make sure they are equal in width and pin as you go.

5 Pin one pleated panel to half of the top of the frame by removing a pin at a time and re-securing it through the pleat and binding. To form the pleats at the bottom, pull the fabric down parallel to the side struts, following the edge of a stripe from a top pleat and pin even pleats around the base, allowing them to fan out. Repeat this process for the other panel on the other half, folding under the raw edges and overlapping the panels where they meet.

equipment, materials, and techniques

Basic sewing kit
To make the projects featured you will need the following: large scissors for cutting paper and card for templates, medium scissors for cutting out fabric, and small embroidery scissors for threads. Pinking shears are useful for neatening raw edges. Choose short, fine, sharp pins and strong needles. An iron is useful for pressing fabric, opening seams and marking pleats. A sewing machine will greatly speed up the process, though it is possible to make these projects by hand if you can sew neatly . Use a safety pin for threading elastic and a blunt knitting needle for pushing out corners.

Measuring and marking tools
Accurate measuring and marking are essential aspects of lampshade making; it is vital to ensure the cover fits neatly onto the frame. Use a metal rule for straight edges and a tape measure for curves and longer lengths. For measuring and drawing small circles use a compass. For larger circles, you can make your own compass using a piece of string. Insert a drawing pin through one end to mark the midpoint of the circle and attach a pencil to the other end. Adjust the length of string according to the diameter you require and pivot the pencil around the pin to draw the circumference. Thick paper or card is ideal for making templates. For some fitted shades and more difficult shapes, it is easier to make the template by pinning a lining material or thin calico directly onto the frame to ensure a close and accurate fit. Use an ordinary pencil, dressmaker's chalk or a removable fabric marker for marking the pattern. ˙

Fixing tools
Work with an appropriate adhesive; use a fabric adhesive for joining fabric to fabric and a multi-purpose glue for attaching all other types of surfaces, such as laminated fabric to a frame. Clothespins are handy for holding glued edges together while drying.

Laminated covers
Stiff covers are made by laminating a fabric with a self-adhesive backing. Slowly peel away the protective paper from the backing and on a flat surface carefully press the wrong side of the fabric to the sticky surface, removing any trapped air by smoothing with your hands from the middle outwards. Stiffen the fabric first and then cut out the required pattern. Self-adhesive backing is not suitable for use on an openweave fabric because dust gathers between the threads.

Fabric covers
The type of material you choose will affect the quality of light shed by the shade. Whites and light plains radiate maximum light, while dark colors and patterns obscure light. Stick to smaller repeats as large-scale patterns will be lost on all but the biggest shades. Lightweight cottons and silks are ideal for tight-fitting shades as they have give in them to aid stretching onto the frame. Geometric patterns such as checks should be cut and applied on the bias (see page 103) as it is difficult to achieve really straight vertical and horizontal lines. By positioning the checks at an angle the eye will not detect a lack of symmetry. Try to use an economical width of fabric for the shade, or piece panels together, pattern matching as necessary.

Fabric will sit better on a shaped frame if it is first cut into smaller pieces and then joined into panels. Pleated and gathered covers are deceptive; they require a lot more fabric than tight covers, often two or three times as much, so calculate amounts carefully and allow for seam allowance when you are joining pieces together.

Frames

There are all manner of shaped frames to choose from. Traditionally, frames were made of wire and then painted or covered with bias binding (see page 101) to prevent rusting, but today most are plastic-coated. When selecting a frame, make sure the style and size are appropriate to the proposed base and fittings. You can re-cover an old frame with new fabric if you strip away the old cover, but make sure there are no defects in the basic outline. Shown opposite are a selection of the most popular frames available with their technical names. You can also buy rings of different diameters, which can be combined with fabrics stiffened by lamination to make cone frames. This method allows for greater flexibility in shape and size than with ready-made wire cone frames.

Linings

These are generally used in white or cream to allow for maximum reflection of light. The lining helps to hide the struts and the outline of the bulb. Use a strong, non-tear and heat-resistant fabric such as fine Shantung or Japanese silk, satin or crepe; an alternative is acetate, although this is more liable to tear. Flame retardant spray is available for treating the lining. No lining is required on a laminated shade or when using very heavy fabrics, but with lightweight fabrics like voile or lace, lining is essential to help diffuse light and give substance to the cover.

Trimmings

Many lampshades are finished with a trimming, to hide unsightly stitching, neaten raw edges and provide decoration. Ball fringes, braid, ribbon, rope, tassels and piping are just some options and they can be glued or hand sewn in place. Measure the section to be trimmed with a tape measure and add at least 1 inch to finish the ends. For removable covers, check the washability and dyes of the trimming. It is a good idea to pre-wash all fabrics and trimmings before starting to assemble the cover, to ensure even shrinkage and to avoid colors bleeding into each other.

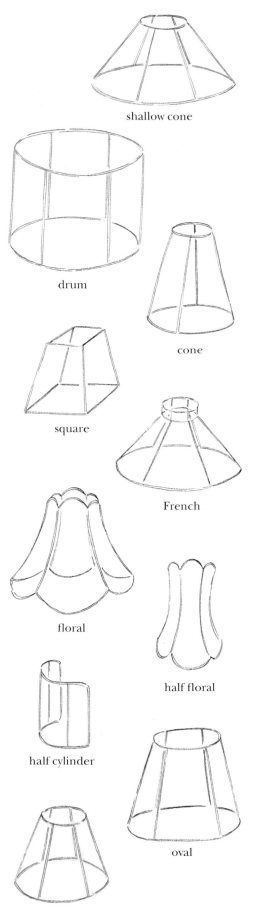

Frames of various shapes:

shallow cone

drum

cone

square

French

floral

half floral

half cylinder

oval

Empire

Fixtures

When you have decided on the size and shape of your frame you must consider the internal fixtures which hold the frame to the support; these are available in various sizes. Your choice of fixture will depend on the function of the shade: for instance a pendant fitting is necessary for hanging shades, whereas a reversible gimbal is used on table lamps, allowing them to be tilted when directing light on specific areas. Converters and shade carriers are available if you wish to change the height or use of your shade. Finally the size of your bulb can affect the fixture – it must be hidden from view and sitting at a safe distance from the lining to avoid scorching or prevent its becoming a fire hazard.

Bulbs

Choose a bulb according to the fixture and the size and style of the shade; the bulb should sit below the level of the top of the shade and not hang below the bottom of the shade. Consumer standards specify the bulb should be a least 1¼ inches away from the inside of the shade. Be extremely careful that the bulb does not come within this recommended distance, or scorching may occur. The bulb must also be set properly in the fixture to avoid burning. For larger lampshades use up to 60-Watt bulb, but on smaller shades choose 40-Watt or below. Low voltage bulbs are long lasting and give off a bright light combined with low heat.

TECHNIQUES

Binding the frame

Binding not only gives a better finish if the shade is seen from above or below but provides a necessary anchor for attaching the fabric cover. In most cases, use a white or neutral binding, although sometimes a different color may suit the design. First make sure the frame is the correct shape and free from bends as any defects will show. Use ½-inch-wide binding tape. To calculate how much tape is needed measure the length of all the sections to be covered and double this measurement. To bind, spiral the tape around the frame maintaining the same angle and just overlapping each previous wrap. Do not overlap by too much or the binding will become very thick. The binding should have a tight, smooth finish so that when you twist it between thumb and index finger it does not slip or move.

To bind a strut, cut a length of binding tape twice the length of the strut. Turn 1 inch of the tape over the top ring and, with the cut end pointing down, spiral the tape downward. Finish at the base of the strut with a simple knot.

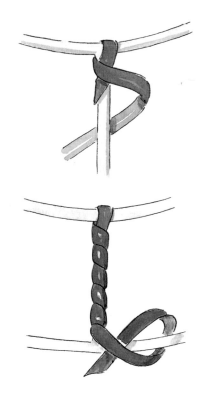

To bind the top and bottom rings of the frame, start by binding a cut end under itself next to a side strut. Where a ring meets a strut work the tape around it in a figure-eight pattern. To finish the loose end, fasten with tiny hand stitches and trim away the excess binding.

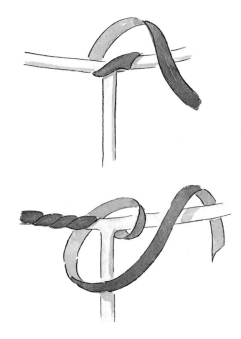

Measuring the frame

To measure any kind of cone-shaped frame, calculate the circumference around the top and bottom of the frame by measuring the relevant diameter and multiplying by three. The height of the frame is the angled (not the vertical) height between the top and bottom rings.

Making a pattern

There are two methods for making your own pattern for covering any cone-shaped frame. You can use the more exact mathematical method, involving a series of intersecting lines, as shown on pages 33 and 91. Or use this alternative method: lay a sheet of paper flat and secure the four corners by pinning to a suitable surface. Place the bare frame in one corner of the sheet, start at one strut and roll the frame across the paper in an arc until the same strut makes contact with the sheet. Rolling slowly, mark the top and bottom arcs with a pencil. Decide on a suitable all around seam allowance. Cut out the paper pattern and check its fit against the frame.

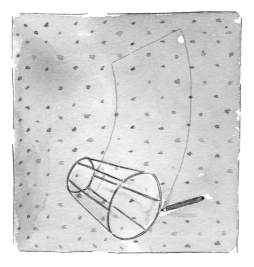

Making a drum

To make a pattern for a drum where the top and bottom rings are the same size, draw a rectangle onto a sheet of paper. The short sides correspond to the height of the shade and the long sides to the circumference; include an overlap allowance at the side.

(The circumference is three times the diameter.) Cut out the fabric and seam allowance. To glue the side of a laminated drum or cone, lie the shade seam down, place a ruler along it and overlay with a few heavy books. Leave to dry in this position.

SEWING TECHNIQUES

Running stitch

A series of small, neat hand stitches equal in length on both sides of the fabric. Knot the ends to secure. Also used to gather cloth. For thicker fabrics and as a security against the thread breaking, sew two close parallel rows of stitches, wind the loose threads at each end around a pin and pull gently to form even gathers.

Slipstitch

Use this almost invisible stitch to join two folded edges or to attach trimmings. Knot the ends of the thread to secure. Working from right to left insert the needle and slip it through the folded fabric for about ⅛inch, then pick up a couple of threads on the opposite fabric to join the two edges.

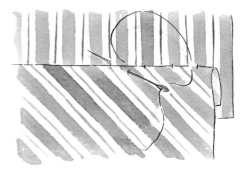

Hemstitch

Use to join fabric to binding tape on a frame or to hold a folded edge to a flat fabric, for example to finish a hem by hand. Catch a couple of threads from the flat fabric, with the needle pointing diagonally from right to left slide it under the fabric or opposite edge and bring it up through all layers.

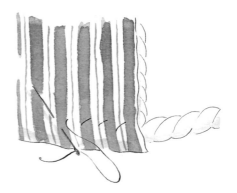

Backstitch

A continuous line of hand stitches, used as an alternative to machine stitching. Sew a line of equal straight stitches from front to back, but start each stitch by inserting the needle halfway through the previous one.

Finishing seams

On fabric not liable to fray either leave the seam allowance untrimmed or pink the raw edges with pinking shears. Otherwise finish a raw edge by oversewing or by machine with a zigzag or overlocking stitch; keep all stitches small and running over the raw edge.

French seam

This makes a very strong seam which is suitable for lightweight fabrics. Place the pieces of fabric to be joined wrong sides together with raw edges matching. Pin, baste and machine a seam ½ inch from the raw edge and trim. Turn the fabric so the right sides are now facing and press the seam line on the fold. Machine a second seam parallel to the first to enclose the raw edges. Press the seam to one side.

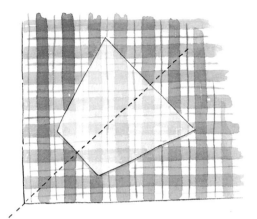

Making bias binding

Bias binding is a strip of fabric cut on the bias or diagonal grain. It is available readymade but you can create much more versatile trimmings yourself by making your own. Make sure that purchased bias binding is shrinkproof and colorfast before sewing. To make bias strips find the bias line (see below) and use a long ruler and a pencil to mark out a series of lines parallel to the bias line, according to the width you need.

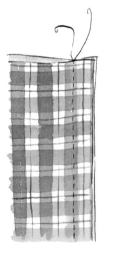 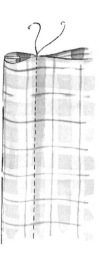

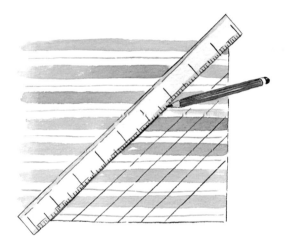

Cutting fabric on the bias

For tight covers you should cut fabric out on the bias; fabric used in this way has greater give and better stretch than fabric cut out horizontally with the direction of the grain. Before you start, make sure the fabric lends itself to this technique; some patterns may not match neatly across the angled seam produced by this method. To find the bias, take a square of fabric and fold a straight raw edge parallel to the selvage (the non-fray woven edge), so forming a triangle. The long bottom edge of the triangle is the bias line, or true direction of bias on the fabric. Line your template up so that the bias line runs straight through the shape.

To make the long lengths that are usually required, cut out and join the bias strips along the short ends by placing them rights sides together; using a diagonal rather than a vertical seam means the strip will have greater flexibility for trimming. Note that there is a useful tool for making bias binding available from notions departments.

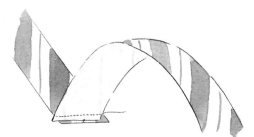

directory of suppliers

fabrics and trimmings

Laura Ashley
414 Madison Avenue,
New York, NY 10021

Beacon Hill
979 Third Avenue,
New York, NY 10022

Bennison Fabrics
76 Greene Street,
New York, NY 10012

***Boussac of France**
979 Third Avenue,
New York, NY 10022

***Alan Campbell**
979 Third Avenue,
New York, NY 10022

***Manuel Canovas**
979 Third Avenue,
New York, NY 10022

Clarence House
211 East 58th Street,
New York, NY 10022

***Jane Churchill
Fabrics & Wallpapers**
distributed by
Cowtan & Tout,
979 Third Avenue,
New York, NY 10022

***Colefax & Fowler**
distributed by
Cowtan & Tout,
979 Third Avenue,
New York, NY 10022

***Coraggio Textiles**
979 Third Avenue,
New York, NY 10022

***Cowtan & Tout**
979 Third Avenue,
New York, NY 10022

Pierre Deux
870 Madison Avenue,
New York, NY 10003

***Designers Guild**
distributed by Osborne &
Little, 979 Third Avenue,
New York, NY 10022

***Donghia**
979 Third Avenue,
New York, NY 10022

***Decorator's Walk**
979 Third Avenue,
New York, NY 10022

***Fortuny**
979 Third Avenue,
New York, NY 10022

***Pierre Frey**
distributed by Fonthill,
979 Third Avenue,
New York, NY 10022

Giant Textiles
P.O. Box 84228,
Seattle, WA 98124

***S.Harris & Co.
/Fabricut**
979 Third Avenue,
New York, NY 10022

***Hinson & Co.**
979 Third Avenue,
New York, NY 10022

***Christopher Hyland**
979 Third Avenue,
New York, NY 10022

***Lee Jofa**
979 Third Avenue,
New York, NY 10022

***Kirk-Brummel
Associates**
979 Third Avenue,
New York, NY 10022

***Kravet Fabrics Inc.**
979 Third Avenue,
New York, NY 10022

***Calvin Klein Home**
654 Madison Avenue,
New York, NY 10022

Jack Lenor Larsen
41 East 11th Street,
New York, NY 1003-4685

Ralph Lauren Home
*979 Third Avenue,
New York, NY 10022
980 Madison Avenue,
New York, NY 10021
867 Madison Avenue,
New York, NY 10021

*Osborne & Little
979 Third Avenue,
New York, NY 10022

*Payne Fabrics, Inc.
979 Third Avenue,
New York, NY 10022

**Ian Mankin at
Coconut Co.**
129-31 Greene Street,
New York NY 10012-8080

***Quadrille Wallpapers
& Fabrics**
979 Third Avenue,
New York, NY 10022

Randolph & Hein
1 Arkansas Street,
San Francisco, CA 94107

*Sanderson
979 Third Avenue,
New York, NY 10022

Scalamandre
942 Third Avenue,
New York, NY 10022

Schumacher Intl. Ltd.
939 Third Avenue,
New York, 10022

**J.Robert Scott
& Associates**
979 Third Avenue,
New York, NY 10022

Sonia's Place
979 Third Avenue,
New York, NY 10022

Stroheim & Romann
31 Thomson Avenue,
Long Island City, NY
11101

**Jim Thompson/Zimmer
Rohde**
979 Third Avenue,
New York, NY 10022

Westgate Fabrics
979 Third Avenue,
New York, NY 10022

lampshades

*Abat Jour
232 East 59th Street,
New York, NY 10022

Laura Ashley
714 Madison Avenue,
New York, NY 10021

Crate & Barrel
650 Madison Avenue,
New York, NY 10022

Lee Garvey
401 East 88th Street,
New York, NY 10128

Grand Brass Lamp Parts
221 Grand Street,
New York, NY

Just Shades
21 Spring Street, New
York, NY 10013

***Lacey's Custom
Lampshades**
7320 Ashcroft, Suite 301,
Houston, Texas 77081

Oriental Lampshade
816 Lexington Avenue,
New York, NY 10021

Vaughan
979 Third Avenue,
New York, NY 10022

Ruth Vitow
351 East 61st Street,
New York, NY 10021

* denotes trade only;
contact the address given
for your nearest supplier

credits

front cover: from top to bottom: fabric Ian Mankin; fabric Pierre Frey, trimming Colefax &
Fowler; fabric Pierre Frey; solid red silk Brunschwig & Fils, striped silk Manuel
Canovas; fabric Pierre Frey; all shades made by Vaughan
page 1 checked and solid thin silk taffeta shade by Anna Thomas
page 2 from top to bottom: shade made by Sally Harclerode, fabric from Designers Guild,
piping from V.V.Rouleaux; shade made by Bella Figura, fabric from Baer & Ingram,
trimming from Jane Churchill ; shade made by Sally Harclerode, fabric from Osborne
& Little; shade made by Robert Wyatt, fabric from Ian Mankin
page 4 from left to right: shade made by Robert Wyatt, ribbon by V.V. Rouleaux; shade made
by Acres Farm, fabric from Ian Mankin; shade made by Robert Wyatt
page 5 from left to right: shade by Vaughan, fabric from Manuel Canovas; shade by Vaughan,
fabric from Manuel Canovas; shade by Robert Wyatt, fabric from Sanderson, leather
from John Lewis
page 6 shade made by Robert Wyatt, fabric from JAB, trimming from V. V. Rouleaux
page 7 clockwise from bottom left: shade made by Tindle, fabric from Jane Churchill; shade
made by Robert Wyatt, fabric from Design Archives; shade made by Robert Wyatt,
fabric from Sanderson; shade made by Vaughan, fabric from Jane Churchill ; shade
made by Robert Wyatt, fabric from Designers Guild; shade made by Vaughan, fabric
from Sanderson

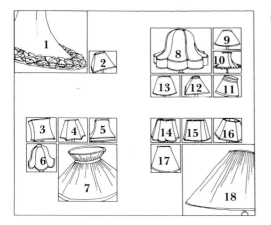

shapes pages 8–9
1 shade from Renwick & Clarke
2, 4, 9, 11, 13,18 silk shades from Vaughan
3, 10 silk shade from Renwick & Clarke
5, 8, 12, 14, 15, 16, 17 silk shades from Tindle
6 silk shade from Lion Witch & Lampshade
7 silk shade from Sally Harclerode

projects: *laminated checked square:* made by Robert Wyatt. base from Hannah Gordon Designs, fabric from The Blue Door • *pleated silk:* made by Sally Harclerode, silk from Pongees *tall madras bowed oval:* made by Robert Wyatt, fabric from JAB, trimming by V. V. Rouleaux

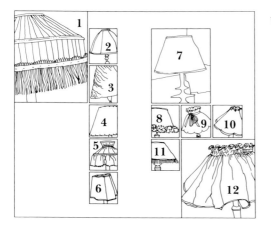

use of fabrics and trimmings pages 22–23
1, 3, 5 silk shades from Lion Witch & Lampshade
2 shade made by Robert Wyatt, fabric from Ian Mankin
4 shade from Patrick Quiggly
6, 9 shades from Vaughan
7 shade from Vaughan, fabric Ian Mankin
8 shade from Renwick & Clarke
10 shade from The Dining Room Shop
11 shade made by Sally Harclerode, fabric from Manuel Canovas, trimming from Osborne & Little
12 shade made by Sally Harclerode, fabric from Designers Guild, piping from V. V. Rouleaux

projects: *skirted pictorial print:* made by Bella Figura, fabric from Baer & Ingram, trimming from Jane Churchill • *burlap half shade:* made by Robert Wyatt • *raw and ruffled:* shade from Renwick & Clarke • *woven ribbons:* made by Robert Wyatt, ribbon from V. V. Rouleaux • *tutu in voile:* shade from Vaughan

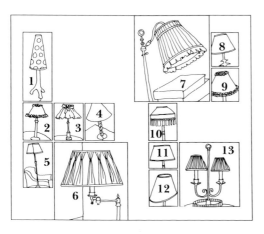

table lamps pages 44–45
1 shade made by Robert Wyatt, fabric from Designers Guild, base from Hannah Gordon Designs
2 Renwick & Clarke shade, base Heal's
3 shade and base from Elizabeth Eaton
4 shade made by Robert Wyatt, fabric from Design Archives, base from Vaughan
5 shade from Tindle, fabric from Jane Churchill, base from Besselink & Jones
6 shade and base from Besselink & Jones
7 shade and base from Vaughan
8 shade from Vaughan, base from Hannah Gordon Designs
9, 11 shades from Besselink & Jones
10 shade made by Sally Harclerode, fabrics and trimmings from Osborne & Little
13 shades and base by Vaughan, fabric from Sanderson

projects: *box-pleated conical shade:* fabric from Manuel Canovas, base and shade by Vaughan • *smocked patterned shade:* shade from The Dining Room Shop • *covered shade:* shade from Vaughan • *scalloped crown:* made by Robert Wyatt, fabric from The Blue Door

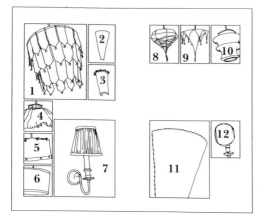

wall and ceiling lamps pages 62–63
1 shade from Nimbus Designs
2, 11 shade from Patrick Quiggly
3 shade made by Robert Wyatt, fabric from Chelsea Textiles, fringe from Osborne & Little
4 shade made by Vaughan, fabric from Celia Birtwell
5 shade by Robert Wyatt
6 shade by Robert Wyatt, burlap from B. Brown
7 shade and wall bracket from Vaughan, fabric from Sanderson
8 shade from Mr. Light
9, 10 shade from Extraordinary Design
12 shade made by Tindle, fabric from Chelsea Textiles

projects: *linen loose cover:* made by Hänsi Schneider, fabric from Sahco Hesslein • *gingham in gathers:* shade by Vaughan, fabric from Ian Mankin, trimming from V. V. Rouleaux • *chandelier candle shades:* shades made by Acres Farm, fabric from Ian Mankin • *two-tiered hanging lamp:* from The Blue Door • *striped wall shield:* shade by Sally Harclerode, fabric from Manuel Canovas

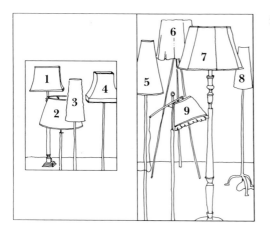

floor lamps pages 84–85
1 shade made by Robert Wyatt, fabric by Schumacher for Turnell & Gigon, trimming from Liberty, base from Vaughan
2 shade made by Bella Figura, fabric from Monkwell., base from Bella Figura
3 shade and base from Mr Light
4 shade from Tindle, base from Mr Light
5 shade made by Robert Wyatt, fabric from JAB, base from Mr Light
6 shade and base from Purves & Purves
7 shade made by Bella Figura, fabric from Parkertex, base from Vaughan
8 shade and base from Mr. Light
9 shade made by Vaughan, fabric from Knickerbean, base from Bella Figura

projects: *stripes around a drum:* made by Robert Wyatt, fabric from Monkwell, trimming from Jane Churchill, base from Habitat • *leather-stitched chimney:* made by Robert Wyatt, fabric from Sanderson, leather from John Lewis • *pleated cone with collar:* made by Vaughan, fabric from Manuel Canovas

page 98   shade from Besselink & Jones
page 99   all shades made by Robert Wyatt, green fabric from John Stefanidis, red fabric from The Blue Door, purple fabric from Manuel Canovas
page 104   shade from The Blue Door
page 105   shade made by Sally Harclerode, fabric from Designers Guild, base from Besselink & Jones
page 109   shade made by Sally Harclerode, fabric from Designers Guild, piping from V. V. Rouleaux, base from The Blue Door
page 110   shade from Renwick & Clarke
page 111   shade from Renwick & Clarke
page 112   shade and base by Robert Wyatt, fabric from Ian Mankin, ball fringe from Jane Churchill
endpapers: shade made by Vaughan, fabric from Colefax & Fowler

glossary

Ball fringe
Tufted ball attached to a length
of trimming.

Basting
Large straight stitches used to
fasten layers of fabric in position
temporarily.

Basting thread
Also tacking thread. Usually
made of cotton and worked in a
loose stitch. Use a contrasting
color to show up against your
fabric.

Bias binding tape or strip
Also crossway strip: a strip cut
obliquely from selvage to selvage
for added strength. Used to bind
frames, edges or to enclose
piping cord.

Box pleat
A symmetrical pleat with fabric
turned in at each side.

Braid
A woven ribbon used to trim or
edge pillows.

Burlap
A strong, coarse fabric made of
jute or hemp fibres. Most commonly used for sacking and in
upholstery.

Casing
An enclosing cover used for
both decorative and protective
purposes.

Gathers
Puckers or folds made in cloth
by drawing on a loosely stitched
thread.

Gimbal fitting
The device attached to the
inside of a frame; used to fit the
shade to the base and the bulb.

Gimp
A twist of fabric, sometimes
stiffened with cord or wire.

Gingham
A fine cotton cloth of Indian

origin usually woven in stripes or
checks.

Grain
The pattern of lines on a fabric,
according to the weave.

Hem
A border or cut edge of cloth,
usually turned under and sewn
in place.

Hole punch
Special tool used to pierce holes
in a material.

Interfacing
Special material used to line and
stiffen a fabric; either sewn or
ironed in place.

Knife-pleat
A narrow sharply folded pleat
with a straight edge.

Laminate
A thin protective covering,
bonded to a material.

Leather thong
A narrow strip of leather used as
a lace.

Madras cotton
Striped and checked fine Indian
cotton, commonly identified by
its bright colors.

Notch
A small V-shaped cut into the
edge of a fabric.

Organza
A thin, transparent, plain-woven
silk or synthetic fabric with a stiff
finish.

Pinking shears
Scissors with notched blades
used for cutting a zigzag edge
for decoration or finishing.

Pleat
A double fold or crease, pressed
or stitched in place.

Provençal print
French country print on
cotton, characterized by small
brightly coloured motifs.

Raw edge
The cut edge of fabric, without
selvage or hem; often needs finishing to prevent fraying.

Ruffle
A gathered strip of cloth used as
a trimming.

Score
To mark a line by scratching the
surface.

Seam allowance
The narrow strip of raw-edged
fabric left when making a seam,
to allow for fraying.

Seam line
The line formed when two
pieces of material are stitched
together.

Selvage
The defined warp edge of the
fabric, specially woven to
prevent unravelling.

Snip
A small cut made in a piece of
material with scissors.

Strut
A bar fitted into a frame to
strengthen against pressure.

Template
A shape made of card or paper,
used to mark specific outlines
on fabric.

Toile
Plain cloth on its own or in *toile
de Jouy* to mean fabric
embellished with pictorial
scenes.

Undershade
A shade usually made of stiff
card and used as a base for a
more decorative outer covering.

Width
The distance from selvage to
selvage on any fabric. The
standard widths for fabric are
36 inches, 45 inches and
60 inches.

index

acknowledgements

Many, many thanks to all the suppliers who so kindly helped us with this book:
all the fabric companies who gave us their gorgeous fabrics and trimmings, all
those who lent us lamp bases and shades. To Lucy Vaughan and all who work at
Vaughan, I thank for all their patience and help while I drove them crazy
borrowing their lovely lamps and shades. To Robert Wyatt for all his great ideas
and lampshades and help on the technical side – many thanks. Sally Harclerode
made some exquisite shades for us – thank you. And to Betty Hanley, the
doyenne of beautiful lampshades, who is now retired but by whose training
many people are still producing bespoke lampshades.

Thanks to Annie Stevens and Anna Thomas for letting us invade their houses to
take many of the photographs; to Catherine Coombes who tirelessly helped
with this book and kept everyone at home happy at the same time; to James
Merrell for his gorgeous photographs; to a really great and professional team at
Ryland Peters & Small – well done; to David and
Harry always and forever.

dedication

In memory of my father and Carolyn Brunton